The 95th (Rifles) in America

UNIFORM OF THE 95TH

The 95th (Rifles) in America

The experiences of two soldiers
during the War of 1812

Harry Smith and William Surtees
—with accompanying histories by—
Eric Sheppard and William Cope

LEONAUR

The 95th (Rifles)
in America
The experiences of two soldiers during the War of 1812
Harry Smith and William Surtees
with accompanying histories of the campaign
and regiment in the period by
Eric Sheppard and William Cope

FIRST EDITION

Leonaur is an imprint
of Oakpast Ltd

Copyright in this form © 2010 Oakpast Ltd

ISBN: 978-0-85706-186-7(hardcover)
ISBN: 978-0-85706-185-0 (softcover)

http://www.leonaur.com

Publisher's Notes

Contents

Publishers Introduction

While there is, undoubtedly, much interest in the activities of Wellington's green jacketed sharpshooters—the famous Rifles—during the Napoleonic period, the focus of that interest lies, for many, in the regiment's service in Portugal and Spain during the Peninsular War against Napoleon's invading French Army, and as the 95th later fought at Quatre Bras and Waterloo in 1815, as the Emperor—lately absconded from exile on the island of Elba—was finally bought to ruin and with his ruin an end to the epoch of war and bloodshed that now bears his name.

But these were not the only campaigns that required the services of the men with the Baker Rifles. They had seen action in Holland, Denmark, Germany and South America in dozens of engagements where their unique expertise and élan could be effectively employed.

In 1814, as the war in Europe ended after Toulouse, and the Bourbon king was once again reinstated on the throne of France, all believed the 'Old World' would now enjoy a quiet period of peace and restoration. However, Britain had business yet unfinished across the Atlantic Ocean in the 'New World.'

The animosity of the new nation of the United States of America had flared into open hostilities with the War of 1812. Now that the great threat of Imperial France—just a short sail across the English Channel—was apparently gone forever, it was time for England to divert the expert and seasoned veterans of 'the Old Peninsula Army that could go anywhere and do anything' to a new theatre of war in its former colonies.

Several regiments were dispatched to America and among them were elements of the 95th (Rifles). The Rifles have fortunately left posterity a larger than usual array of personal military memoirs by the officers and ordinary soldiers of the regiment. However, as one might expect, most of them concentrate on those campaigns were the regiment was principally and consistently engaged. Just two deal the expedition to America in part—those of Harry Smith—at the time a major—and Quartermaster William Surtees.

Leonaur has published most—if not all—of the accounts written concerning the Napoleonic period by Riflemen. The Leonaur Editors are aware that most students of military history tend to focus on periods of time, most notably defined by the wars and campaigns within them. Despite his brief sojourn on Elba, in the minds of many the Napoleonic era did not end until the Emperor abdicated for a second time after his flight from defeat on the slopes before Mont St Jean. So the expedition to America, although a true war of the Napoleonic period, is something of a diversion—another war against another enemy that does not quite 'fit.'

That is why in Leonaur books by Riflemen who served in America, this aspect of their military experience has been excised in the interests of cohesion and to provide modern readers with books on subjects that in their entirety are what we believed our readers wanted.

Of course, we always knew there was a place for a book about the Rifles and the War of 1812. The conflict has its own students and we have, over the last few years, received several requests to cover the subject utilising the excised material. This is that book.

The Smith and Surtees accounts are substantial but do not, on their own, constitute a full length book even when combined. So we have elected to include Eric Sheppard's concise overview of the total conflict and, taken from the Leonaur edition of William Cope's *History of the 95th (Rifles)*, the passage which specifically deals with the activities of the regiment in the

War of 1812, most notably the debacle for the British which was the Battle of New Orleans.

As most students know this was bloodshed that need never have taken place since peace had been negotiated already. So the two personal accounts here end abruptly. Surtees' days of active service were all but over and Major Smith found himself hurrying back to his regiment in Belgium there to join them as brigade-major on the ridge before Waterloo. His experiences in the Peninsula and at Waterloo can be found in the Leonaur book *Bugler and Officer of the Rifles*, (a 2-in1 volume with bugler William Green's Peninsula experiences). William Surtees account of his war in the Peninsula can be found in *Surtees of the Rifles*, also published by Leonaur.

The Leonaur Editors

An Overview of the War With the United States, 1812-1815— Eric Sheppard

Simultaneously with the Titanic struggle with Napoleonic France, Great Britain became involved in the summer of 1812 in a second conflict with a great Power—one which in less strenuous days would have absorbed all her energies, but was regarded apparently by contemporaries, and certainly by posterity, as merely a "side show" to the greater events of the time in Europe.

The causes of dispute which finally arrayed England and the United States against each other had been long outstanding, in fact, ever since the former Power's declaration of war with France in 1803, and were the result of the strenuous commercial conflict in which England was engaged and our infringement of what Americans considered to be their rights as neutrals. It was most unfortunate, however, for the States that they only resolved—owing largely to skilful French diplomacy— to appeal to arms when the Napoleonic Empire, long past its zenith, was about to take its first plunge into disaster, and when affairs in the Peninsula had turned decidedly in favour of Great Britain.

When war finally broke out in July 1812, the first and most obvious objective for the armies and fleets of the United States was Canada, and it was confidently expected by all Americans that the conquest of this, the most valuable of their enemy's overseas possessions, would be only a military promenade. Indeed it seemed unlikely that Canada, with her weak armed forces, under command of Prevost, numbering barely 22,000, of which only four battalions were British regulars, her sparse population of 400,000, and her undefended frontier of 1400 miles between Lake Superior and the Atlantic coast, could for long make head against the eight millions of her adversary, who could place in the field 36,000 trained and close on 100,000 partly trained men. Nevertheless, the seemingly impossible was accomplished; and the story of this remarkable but forgotten feat of arms must now be briefly narrated.

As about half of the long frontier between the contending armies is formed by the water of the great lakes, the command of these lakes was realised by both sides to be of the highest importance, and was bitterly contested throughout the war. In the earlier stages this command was in the hands of the Canadians, but in view of the superior shipbuilding resources of their adversaries it was at best precarious, and, in fact, was always menaced, and more than once—though never permanently—lost.

The American plan of campaign for 1812 comprised three widely separated attacks, one against Amherstburg, a fortified post on the isthmus between Lakes Huron and Erie; a second against the frontier on the Niagara River, between Lakes Erie and Ontario, and a third by the time-honoured route up Lake Champlain and the Richelieu River against the line of the St. Lawrence between Quebec and Montreal. All three were disastrous failures. The force engaged in the first was defeated and compelled to capitulate in the open field, and though the attack was renewed in January 1813 it met with no better success; while in this sector of the front, more to the north-west, the Canadians scored a subsidiary but important point by the seizure of Fort Mackinac at the north end of Lake Huron, which they held till the close of the war against all efforts to retake it.

The American column operating in the Niagara sector, after establishing itself on the west bank of that river, was thrust back by the local British commander, Brock, who unhappily fell in the moment of victory; while the third expedition in the

Richelieu dwindled away to nothing but a futile demonstration. Only at sea, where the American frigates, in a series of single combats with hostile ships, gained a series of striking and unexpected victories, did any success attend the arms of the United States during this year.

Nevertheless, the main lines of operation for 1813 were as in the previous year, except that the various attacks were to be carried out in greater strength and to be more carefully combined. Moreover, the American flotillas on the lakes were now in a position to render valuable assistance to the land forces. Early in the year the naval control of Lake Ontario was temporarily wrested from the Canadians; an American force was shipped across to raid and burn York (now Toronto), the capital of Upper Canada, and thence sailed to open the campaign on the Niagara front. The Canadians were driven from their fortified posts there and forced to retire westward, and their situation was not improved by the miscarriage of a diversion against the American naval base opposite Kingston. Meanwhile matters had gone even worse on Lake Erie, where the Canadian flotilla had been completely defeated and destroyed, and control of the lake permanently secured by the enemy; this in turn compelled the force holding Amherstburg to evacuate that place and fall back eastwards along the northern shore, during which movement it was caught and completely dispersed.

The situation of Upper Canada was, at this moment, serious, but fortunately, prior to the disaster on Lake Erie, the lost command of Ontario had been regained, and the Americans forced back once more to the Niagara. Nor were they allowed even there to rest in peace; for at the end of the year Drummond, assuming command of the Canadian troops, m a vigorous little campaign first of all swept them from the west bank, and then, crossing over, took and destroyed all their fortifications on the farther shore. Meanwhile, the American offensive against Lower Canada, carried out concentrically by two columns advancing from Lake Champlain and down the St. Lawrence, had also failed, their forces being defeated before they could effect their junction.

1813 had thus brought a real but not decisive advantage to the United States, and this it was intended to exploit and extend in 1814 by a large-scale effort on the Niagara front, combined with subsidiary operations on the flanks against Fort Mackinac and in the Richelieu valley. But meanwhile the British fleet had definitely asserted its supremacy and tightened its blockade of the Atlantic coast, and reinforcements in considerable numbers were on their way to Canada, though the first batch (four battalions) only arrived in July. The Canadians opened the campaign with a successful raid on Oswego on Lake Ontario, while far away in the north-west the American attack on Mackinac was repulsed.

At length, after many delays, the United States forces commenced their offensive in the Niagara sector, but their progress was checked in the hard-fought little action of Lundy's Lane, and they were compelled to retire to their fortifications once more. Drummond, advancing to invest them, was in turn checked, and it was not till the end of the campaigning season that the Americans had to admit failure and withdraw over the river. As some set-off to this a British counter-offensive undertaken by Prevost in person against the hostile forces in Lake Champlain ended, owing to an unfortunate misunderstanding between the sailors and the soldiers, in a humiliating fiasco at Plattsburg; the flotilla was defeated with heavy loss, and the army compelled to withdraw hurriedly to its starting-point.

During the latter course of this year the British had assembled in American waters sufficient armed forces to enable them to take the initiative and open offensive operations against the mainland of the United States. One detachment from Halifax occupied Eastern Maine as far as the Penobscot, and retained it till the peace. Another force of 4000 men under Ross sailed boldly into Chesapeake Bay, marched on Washington and, driving off at Bladensburg the militia who attempted to oppose its advance, occupied the city, and only retired after burning all the public buildings, as a reprisal for the American destruction of

York in the previous year.

Re-embarking, it next assailed Baltimore, but was compelled to withdraw owing to the inability of the fleet to cooperate in the attack on that city. Reinforced to a strength of some 6000, and under a new commander, Pakenham, the little army now undertook a more difficult enterprise against New Orleans, at the mouth of the Mississippi, and with infinite labour was transported by boat to within striking distance of the fortified lines which had been constructed by the Governor of the place, Andrew Jackson, who was later to become President of the United States; but the assault failed with the loss of the British commander and many men, and the force was with difficulty got away, only to be set to undertake a new enterprise against Mobile.

Peace had in actual fact been signed between Great Britain and the United States at Ghent before the disaster at New Orleans, and the news of it reached America just after the forts of Mobile had surrendered. Its terms left the main questions in dispute unsettled, and the futile bloodshed on the Mississippi was a fitting termination to a foolish war which should never have taken place, and of which the main result was to render both belligerents—more especially the United States, the aggressors—weaker and more embittered than before its commencement. Indeed the only people to emerge from it with enhanced credit were the Canadians, who had vindicated their right to national existence by a noteworthy display in arms.

The Service of 95th Rifles
in America—
William Cope

Five companies of the 3rd Battalion, on their return from the Peninsula disembarked at Plymouth, and moved into barracks there. On September 18, 1814, exactly two months after their arrival in England, they re-embarked for service; the commanding officer, Major Mitchell, and three companies on board the *Fox*, and the other two companies on board the *Dover* frigates. Their destination and the nature of their service were kept a profound secret, but they were, in fact, intended to effect a descent on the American coast near New Orleans. They reached Madeira on the 8th October, where they remained till the 11th, and having touched at Barbadoes early in November, anchored in Negril Bay, Jamaica, on the 25th. Here they were joined by four line regiments, and two West India regiments; and setting sail on the 29th, arrived off the American coast near Mobile on December 10, and on the 11th anchored near the Chandeleur Islands near the entrance to Lake Borgne.

New Orleans is situated on the left bank of the Mississippi, here about 800 or 1,000 yards across; below the town are great marshes, covered with reeds six or seven feet high. While on the river bank runs a strip of firm ground, varying from one to three miles across, and mostly under sugar plantations. From this the marsh extends six or seven miles to the shores of Lake Pontchartrain, which communicates by Lake Borgne with the sea.

It was deemed impossible to approach New Orleans by

the Mississippi, as well because very strong works existed at its mouth, and on the way up to the city, as because the course of the river is so tortuous that no wind would have carried the ships up, without considerable delay. It was therefore resolved to disembark the troops on the shore of one of the lakes. But it was ascertained that the Americans, already cognisant of the intended invasion, had placed gun-boats on these lakes to prevent the landing. The previous destruction of these was therefore necessary; and this was effected in very fine style and in a very short time by the boats of the fleet under Captain Lockyer.

On the 15th the Riflemen were moved from the ships of war into brigs, which drew less water, but in which they were so crowded as to be unable to lie down or almost to turn. But even these were too deep for the shoal waters of the lake, and they were transferred into long boats, from which they were landed on the 19th on the Île au Poix (or as our men called it Pearl Island), formed by the branches of the Pearl River. The weather in moving from the ships to the island was very bad; and on arrival at it, it was found to be a perfect desert. Nothing but reeds grew on it, except a few scrubby pine-trees at one end. To add to their discomfort, a severe frost came on at night; the men were without shelter of any kind, and they suffered severely. And as all their supplies had to be furnished from the fleet, want of provisions was added to their other hardships.

On the 22nd the battalion (which formed part of the advance under Colonel Thornton) embarked in boats, and about two o'clock pushed off to land on the mainland. The place decided on for their disembarkation was at the head of a creek called Bayou Catalan in Lake Borgne. The distance was between thirty and forty miles, and the men were so crowded in the boats that they could not move. They did not reach the entrance to the creek till after dark. As a picquet of the enemy was posted about half a mile up the creek. Captain James Travers, with his company, were placed in small boats and pushed forward. The picquet was stationed at some huts; near these Travers landed, and having moved his men to both ends of the huts, prevented the escape of the picquet, which was secured without a shot being fired.

This was admirably effected; and was a most important service. For had this picquet escaped or raised an alarm, the landing would have been opposed. And this would have been a serious check; for on the morning of the 23rd, when the leading boat reached the narrow part of the bayou it was found impracticable to ascend higher, and the boats being drawn up one after another the men passed over them as a bridge. This of course was a very slow operation, and one which, if opposed, would have been very difficult. The battalion disembarked about an hour after daylight, having been upwards of sixteen hours cramped in the boats.

As soon as the whole advance were on shore, they marched, Travers' company leading; and to give their force as imposing an appearance as possible, and to scour the country, they advanced with extended files. They moved in this order through a wood which skirted the swamp on this side, and as soon as they had cleared it, came upon a house, surrounded with out-buildings and huts for slaves, belonging to a M. Villeroy. The battalion advancing at the double, took possession of it; and in this and some neighbouring houses took about thirty prisoners, and a good many stand of arms, belonging, as was supposed, to the local militia.

Unhappily M. Villeroy escaped, and probably gave information to the enemy; this, before the night was over, entailed very disastrous consequences. The battalion then advanced, and turning to the right, marched for about a mile on the road to New Orleans, and then bivouacked in a green field in quarter distance column.

The road ran near the river's bank which was on the left; and an embankment about three or four feet high was thrown up to keep the overflow of the river from the cultivated ground, here about three-quarters of a mile or a mile broad; beyond this was a strip of wood, the way through which was, in fact, impracticable, the ground under the trees being wet and swampy. The cultivated land was much intersected with wet ditches, and divided by strong wooden palings five feet high.

On arriving at the bivouack Travers' company, which had formed the advanced guard on the march, was pushed forward about a mile to the front, on the main road, as a picquet.

The troops halted somewhat after midday; and as the men had been without provisions since the morning before, they began as soon as dismissed to cook. While doing so, between three and four o'clock, firing was heard in the front from the picquet; it turned out to be in consequence of an American officer, attended by some mounted men, riding up to the picquet to reconnoitre. However, the Riflemen saluted him with a few shots, one of which wounded him, and another killed the horse of one of the party, on which they retired, getting off the wounded officer with them.

At nightfall, Captain Hallen's company relieved Travers at the advanced picquet; and the men of the rest of the battalion, being much fatigued by their uncomfortable night in the boats, their tedious landing, and their march, lay down in bivouack. They had torn down some of the palings dividing the fields, and had made good fires which then burned brightly. While they were thus, as they fancied, secure, a schooner dropped down the Mississippi, and guided by the light of their fires, opened a heavy cannonade upon them with great effect. The men of course were aroused and dispersed; but no shelter could be found, in this dead flat, except by crouching under the embankment by the riverside. Hallen had seen the schooner pass his post and had sent a man off to alarm the battalion; but the schooner having the current of the river in her favour reached the bivouack before the Rifleman could get there.

While in this state of alarm from the sudden cannonade from the schooner, heavy and continued firing was heard in the front. A body of 5,000 Americans had attacked Hallen's picquet, detaching 1,500 men through the wood to turn the right of the troops. Nobly Hallen kept them at bay; but being himself wounded, and his picquet threatened by such overpowering odds, reinforcements advanced from the battalion. Meanwhile the enemy made way through the garden of a house on the right, where a picquet of the 85th had been placed; and the night being very dark, a hand to hand fight took place. Every deception was practised by the enemy; and having discovered (from prisoners probably made in the *mêlée*) the regiments opposed to them, they would call out, 'Come on my brave ninety-fifth (or eighty-fifth),' and then make those who advanced prisoners.

But this *ruse* was not always successful; more than once they found that instead of making Riflemen prisoners, they had themselves 'caught a Tartar.' On one such occasion an officer and some men of the battalion made a body of the Yankees prisoners, and when they were desired to lay down their arms, the cowardly officer who commanded them made a stab at the 95th officer with a knife. He was summarily disposed of; for a Rifleman instantly shot him through the body.

Meanwhile the fight continued at Hallen's post. Two battalions came up and fired volleys by word of command as at a drill. Not much to their advantage, for the Riflemen, warned by the words, 'Ready! Present!' took care to lie pretty close before the word 'Fire!' which, having been pronounced and obeyed, they sprang up, and gave them a severe return before they could reload. This continued for some time; but at last, the picquet was obliged to give way before superior numbers. Yet they only retired a little way to get under cover and re-form. Eventually the Riflemen advanced again, attacked their assailants, repulsed them, and regained the post. Hallen, as I have said, was wounded, so was Lieutenant Forbes, who held a separate post, and about forty men were killed or wounded. This defence by Hallen has truly been characterised as 'an affair of posts but rarely equalled, and never surpassed in devoted bravery.' [1]

'Had the expedition terminated more favourably,' he who makes the foregoing remark goes on to observe, 'it is to be presumed that the brave commander of the company would not have gone unrewarded.' It may be so: this is the presumption; the fact is, that Hallen retired from the Service in 1824 with the rank of captain, which he had obtained fifteen years before. Thus England rewarded acts of valour performed by all but her superior officers.

---

1. Leach, *Sketch of Field Services.*.

When the fire was first heard at Hallen's picquet, Major Mitchell, taking with him twenty or thirty Riflemen, had hurried to the front to reinforce it. On the way, however, he fell in with a body of the enemy, whom, in consequence of the darkness of the night, he could not distinguish, and he and the men with him were made prisoners. Altogether the loss of the battalion on that night was six sergeants and seventeen Riflemen killed; Captain Hallen, Lieutenants Daniel Forbes, (severely), and W. S. C. Farmer (slightly), five sergeants and fifty-four Riflemen wounded; and Major Samuel Mitchell, two sergeants, and thirty-nine Riflemen missing. A total (exclusive of officers) of 123, or one-fifth of their whole number.

The loss of the Americans, who were finally driven off about midnight, must have been very great, for the field was strewn with their dead.

Yet still the schooner, and a ship which had joined her, inflicted amazing annoyance on our people. With a brutality happily unknown among European nations, they fired into the houses to which the wounded had been carried. One shot struck a house in which a wounded Rifleman was lying, and knocked away his knapsack, which he was using as a pillow, without doing him any actual injury.

However, this savage warfare was to end. On the night of the 25th a battery was constructed close to the river's edge, and furnaces erected for heating red-hot shot. At daybreak on the 26th the battery commenced its fire on the schooner. Its crew, whose courage did not equal their cruelty, at once took to their boats and fled; the fourth shot set her on fire, and she soon afterwards blew up. While the ship, warned by her fate, and esteeming discretion as the better part of valour, had herself towed, as rapidly as possible, out of the range of the little English battery.

In this bivouack the Riflemen continued till the 28th. But it was toilsome work. The picquets were continually fired at; the reliefs waylaid; the officers going round their sentries exposed to chance shots from a concealed marksman. How different this from the courtesies and chivalry of their European enemies, which I have so often had occasion to narrate!

Early on the 28th the army advanced towards New Orleans, the Riflemen leading, by the high road along the river's bank. They drove in the enemy's picquets, and proceeded along the road here called '*Le détour des Anglais*,' till, on turning round some houses on the left, they suddenly found themselves in front of a strong work the enemy had thrown up, and from which they opened a cannonade from four guns; while their old enemy the ship, now moored a little in advance of the work, brought a flank fire to bear on them. The Riflemen, leading and extended, did not suffer so much;[2] but the 85th which followed in close formation were mown down by this fire.

Some houses were on the right, which might have afforded some temporary cover; but the enemy, by their shells, set them on fire, and the flames added to the confusion. To escape in some measure from the effects of the fire the regiments were deployed to the right, while the Riflemen advancing about a hundred yards got into a ditch, which in a great degree sheltered them. In the afternoon the regiments moved off by wings, so as to present as small a body as possible to the enemy's fire. The Riflemen, however, did not move off till after dark, nor till some of the Yankees had ventured out of their works 'in a very triumphant manner.'

But a few shots from the Riflemen immediately produced the conviction among them that it was more advisable to return to the protection of their rampart. This work was a stout parapet, in front of which was a wet ditch or canal. Its extent was about 1,000 yards, and its left touched the river, while its right was defended by the wood.

The army now took up a position about a mile and a half or two miles from this work. The battalion was placed in a house rather in advance, and on the left of the line. This was exposed, not only to the fire from the work, but also, as it was near the bank, from a redoubt which the enemy had constructed on the opposite side of the river. The men were placed in a sugar-house belonging to this farm, the floor of which being sunk below the

2. Their loss between December 25 and 31 was 1 Rifleman killed; 1 sergeant and 3 Riflemen wounded; and 1 Rifleman missing.

level of the natural ground afforded some protection. Yet on one occasion at least their cooking utensils were knocked off the fire by shot passing through this house.

So matters continued until the 31st. It was resolved to bring up some of the ships' guns and to place them in battery against the enemy's work. Accordingly on the night of the 31st strong working parties were employed in constructing two batteries near it; one with the object of keeping down the flank fire from the ship; the other with the view of breaching the centre of the rampart. The night was dark; the men worked in silence; and before daylight the batteries were completed, and the guns in position.

Early in the morning of January 1, 1815, the troops were moved up, with the object of attacking the enemy's work. A thick fog favoured their advance, and concealed their movements from the Americans. About nine o'clock the fog rose, and our batteries at once began their fire. This threw the Yankees, who were seen on parade, into utter confusion; and had a charge on the works been made at that moment, no doubt it would have been successful. But unhappily the orders were that the attack was not to be made till the enemy's fire had been silenced, and his works breached. When, therefore, the Americans saw that nothing took place but a cannonade, their courage returned, and after about twenty minutes they began to return our fire; and gradually increased to a vigorous cannonade, which effectually overpowered our guns, and dismounted some of them. The flank fire too from the battery on the opposite bank of the river, in which they had placed their ship's guns, was very galling.

After being kept under this fire inactive till between two and three o'clock in the afternoon, the troops were withdrawn and bivouacked on the ground, and some occupied the houses they had held during the last few days. At night the troops were turned out and employed in withdrawing the guns from the batteries in which they had been placed. This was hard work; and some of the guns had to be buried, it being found impossible to remove them before daylight. Thus the men had been up, and at hard work, two nights; and in the intervening day had been for many hours under the enemy's fire, without the chance of fighting them. The loss of the battalion was, one Rifleman killed, and two missing.

Things continued in this state till the 7th, the picquets being as before constantly harassed by the enemy.

No other course remained but to carry the enemy's work by an attack *de vive force*, and it was decided that this should take place on the 8th. Three companies of the battalion were to precede the advance of the right column under General Gibbs, consisting of the 4th, 21st and 44th regiments; while the other two companies were in like manner to act with, the left column. The Riflemen were to extend along the edge of the canal or ditch in front of the enemy's rampart, and both parties so extended were to occupy the whole of the bank, or as it might be called, the crest of the glacis.

At four o'clock in the morning the troops paraded; and by daylight the Riflemen were in their place. But the 44th Regiment, which had been appointed to carry ladders and fascines to enable the attacking force to cross the ditch, had come without them. Their commanding officer, the Hon. Colonel Mullens, had said loudly the night before when the regiment was detailed for this duty in orders, that 'his regiment was sent on a forlorn hope' and 'was doomed.' And on the regiment returning to fetch the ladders and fascines, he prudently did not come back to the front with them.

The enemy meanwhile opened a furious fire on the troops, specially destructive to the Riflemen who were extended within 100 or 150 yards of the work. One regiment of the right attack, finding itself exposed to this fire, and without the fascines and ladders they had been led to expect, wavered, broke up, and fled to the rear, throwing the regiment which was following in support into confusion. Sir Edward Pakenham, who commanded, in trying to rally this column was killed; General Gibbs, who commanded it, was mortally wounded; and General Keane, who commanded the left attack, was wounded.

This attack succeeded better; and for a time the troops composing it held a redoubt which the enemy had constructed in front of the ditch, and which they had stormed. But in the end they were obliged also to give way. Thus the Riflemen, extended in skirmishing order along the edge of the ditch, were left unsupported, and were obliged to retire as best they could. As their files were extended they presented a less prominent object for the enemy's guns, and they eventually got away with comparatively small loss. Some of them had got quite to the edge of the ditch, and reported that they could have passed it, but the attacking columns which they expected never came up; and to have entered the enemy's work without them would, of course, have been certain destruction.

A gallant and successful diversion was made on the right bank of the Mississippi by a column under Colonel Thornton; but as the battalion did not form part of it, it is not my province, as historian of the regiment only, farther to notice it.

It was regretted by the Riflemen, that Pakenham, himself a Peninsular soldier, did not employ troops who had seen fighting more prominently in so arduous an operation as storming this work. The 7th and 43rd had arrived just before; beside both these regiments the Riflemen had fought in Spain and Portugal; the latter were especially companions in arms, and they had hailed their advent with delight. Yet these he held in reserve, while he advanced comparatively unseasoned troops to the fire of the Americans.

The battalion retired at last, sorrowful and weary, to its bivouack. It lost one sergeant and ten Riflemen killed; and Captains James Travers (severely) and Nicholas Travers (slightly), Lieutenants John Reynolds, Sir John Ribton, John Gossett, William Backhouse, and Robert Barker (severely), five sergeants and eighty-nine Riflemen wounded.[3]

During the night the wounded were removed, and a truce for two days, to enable the dead to be buried and the wounded cared for, was made between General Lambert (who succeeded to the command) and General Jackson who commanded the

---

3. Major James Travers, K.H., died February 5, 1841. The ball received at New Orleans had never been extracted, and is said eventually to have caused his death. Lieutenant Backhouse died of his wounds.

American force. This truce was effected, not without difficulty, by Major Harry Smith, assistant adjutant-general, who passed and repassed frequently between the opposing armies.

During this truce every attempt was made by the Yankees to induce our men to desert. The non-commissioned officers were promised commissions, the men land, if they would enter the American service. On one such occasion two sergeants and a private of the 95th were accosted by an officer of American Artillery, who with such large promises invited them to enter the American service. The Riflemen heard the tempter out; and then, in language perhaps rather forcible than complimentary, assured him that they would rather be privates in their own corps, than officers with such 'a set of ragamuffins' as they saw before them; assuring him that if he did not move off, he should have a taste of their rifles. On that hint, he fled; but getting into the work turned a gun on them and fired, knocking over the private, whom however he only wounded.

A Rifleman on sentry was exposed to the solicitations of another of these gentry. He heard all his generous offers of money, land, and promotion; but pretending he did not, he begged him to come a little nearer and 'tell him all about it' The Yankee elated at his success walked up to the post, and when he was well within range, the Rifleman levelled and shot him in the arm. Then walking forward, he led him prisoner to the guard-room; on the way informing him what a real soldier thought of such sneaking attempts on his fidelity.[4]

These attempts were not always unsuccessful, and much desertion took place; but Surtees records with natural pride, that as far as he knew not a single instance took place among the Riflemen of the 3rd Battalion.

During this truce an officer of the American army was observed plundering a wounded soldier. This excited the ire of Corporal Scott of the 3rd Battalion, who (with the permission of his officer) took a shot at the marauder, and tumbled him over

---

4. Gleig, *Campaigns of the British Army at Washington and New Orleans* p. 186. He regrets that he has forgotten, or did not know, the name of this soldier; a regret in which all Riflemen will join.

the man he was plundering.

The last duties having been paid to the dead, and all the wounded that were capable of being moved having been withdrawn, a retreat was effected on the night of the 18th. The fires were trimmed, and the men fell in and marched in silence. The weather had latterly broken up; heavy rains by day, and sometimes thunderstorms, were often followed by frost at night. As it was impossible, owing to the narrowness and shallow water of the Bayou Catalan, to embark the troops where they had landed, a road, or an attempt at a road, had been constructed across the marsh, from the great road to New Orleans, along the river's bank to the shore of Lake Borgne.

This extended some miles, and was made of reeds, which it was thought would support the men across the morass; and where it crossed open ditches, as it frequently did, the reeds were laid on boughs of trees brought with great labour from the wood. This road, a bad one at the best, was much injured by the rains, and sunk in with the tramp of the head of the column; so that this night march was very fatiguing, the men often sinking in to the knees, and sometimes in the dark slipping off into the marsh, from whence they were with difficulty rescued.

However at last on the 19th they reached the shore of the lake about one mile from its entrance. Here they were ordered to hut themselves; but this was no easy task, the place being a desert, and almost the only material the reeds which grew on the marsh.

Here they remained till the 25th, when the battalion embarked on board the *Dover*, which had brought out two of its companies. The battalion was reduced by its losses in the field to almost half its strength on landing. On the 27th they set sail; and it was resolved to attempt the capture of Mobile. This place, lying about 100 miles to the eastward of New Orleans, is situated in a bay, the entrance to which is defended by a work called Fort Boyer, which therefore had first to be reduced. In order to effect this the 4th, 21st, and 44th Regiments were landed, and commenced the investment of and approach to the place. While on the 8th February the Riflemen and the rest of the troops were disembarked on Île Dauphine at the other side of the bay, till the reduction of Fort Boyer should enable them to move up to Mobile. Here the men hutted themselves; for the island, though otherwise almost a desert, is well covered with pine wood; while the officers, or some of them, had tents.

During the time that they were here. General Lambert inspected the troops by regiments. On making his inspection of the 3rd Battalion, James Travers (in Mitchell's absence, who had been taken prisoner) was in command. 'Well, Travers,' said the general, 'I hear your sergeant-major ran away on the night of the 23rd December.'

'Nay, General,' answered Travers, 'that he did not. He fought as well as any man could, and was towards the end of the affair severely wounded. But,' added. he, 'I think I know what may have given rise to that report. A sergeant of ours was in or near one of the houses where the wounded were taken, and the surgeon made him remain there as hospital sergeant. I did all I could to get him back to the battalion; but I could not succeed.'

'Well,' said the general, 'since I had done the sergeant-major some wrong, I must see what I can do to make him amends.' He did procure him an ensigncy in a West India Regiment, to which he was gazetted soon after.

While the battalion was on Île Dauphine, a gallant act was performed by Sergeant Thomas Fukes. He, with four or five Riflemen, was sent over to the mainland to shoot bullocks. Fukes with a couple of Riflemen went inland, leaving the other men in charge of the boat. Here one Shiel of the American navy (who had captured a boat in bad weather with some of the 14th Light Dragoons, when embarking at Lake Borgne, and who in consequence fancied himself a hero) came upon them round a jutting point, and having captured them, put them in charge of some of his own crew into their own boat, and dispatched them to an American ship or post.

Then waiting for the sergeant, the other two Riflemen, and the commissary, he of course made them prisoners, since their boat and the rest of their party had disappeared. The commissary was placed aft with Mr. Shiel; Sergeant Fukes and his two men forward; and they were being rowed off. When well off the shore the commissary seizing Shiel by the thighs chucked him overboard, while Sergeant Fukes at the same instant sent one of the boat's crew to follow him, and the Riflemen disposed of the rest. They now recovered their rifles, and having taken security of Mr. Shiel for his good behaviour, admitted him at his urgent importunity into the boat, from whence they landed him, a moist and dispirited prisoner of war, on Île Dauphine.

The approaches to Fort Boyer being completed, Harry Smith was sent in with a summons to surrender. The poor Yankee commandant, sadly puzzled, asked Major Smith what he would advise him to do. He strongly recommended him to surrender immediately, as the place must be taken by assault. Acting on such good advice, which fell in probably with his own sinking courage, he surrendered with his garrison, and signed a capitulation on the 11th February.

This important work having fallen, immediate preparations were made for re-embarking the troops, and attacking Mobile. But on the 14th news arrived of the preliminaries of peace between England and the United States having been settled at Ghent on December 24. All warlike operations of course terminated; and the troops only awaited on Île Dauphine the ratification of the treaty by President Madison. Intelligence of this reached them on the 5th March, and on the 15th the officers and Riflemen who had been made prisoners rejoined the Battalion, having been released under the terms of the treaty. Major Mitchell had been roughly treated by General Jackson, because he refused to furnish him with information of our strength or movements.

On the 31st March the battalion embarked on board the *Dover*, some few men being placed on board the *Norfolk* transport. On the 4th April they set sail, and, having called at the Havannah, arrived at Plymouth, whence they were ordered round to Dover, where they disembarked on the 2nd June and moved to Shornclifife, where they found three companies of the battalion, the remaining two being in Flanders.

Quarter-Master Surtees
of the 95th Rifles in America

EMBARK FOR AMERICA

We embarked (at the close of the European War) on the 8th
July on board His Majesty's ship *Dublin*, of 74 guns, commanded
by Captain Elphinstone, which took the five companies of my
battalion, with two companies of the 43rd. We sailed the next
day, I think, and had generally fine weather during our voyage,
which lasted till the 18th, when we arrived at Plymouth. She
was but a dull sailer, or we ought not to have occupied so many
days in so short a passage. During our voyage, as remarkable an
instance of heroic fortitude and bodily strength was exhibited
by a sailor of this ship as I ever remember to have witnessed. He
was doing something on the fore-yard, and by some accident he
was precipitated into the water, but in his full his shoulder came
in contact with the flue of one of the anchors, by which it was
deeply and severely cut.

The ship was going at about five knots an hour, and it took
near half an hour before she could be brought round and a
boat sent to his assistance; and notwithstanding the severe cut
he had received, from which the blood was fast streaming, he
not only contrived to keep himself from sinking by buffeting
with a heavy sea, but actually stripped off his jacket in the water,
as it seems it had been an encumbrance to him. When the boat
reached him, the poor fellow was nigh exhausted, and a few
minutes more would have deprived the ship and the service of

an excellent sailor, but having been got into the boat, he was brought, on board more dead than alive, where every attention being paid to him, he soon afterwards recovered.

We landed at Plymouth on the 18th, and occupied one of the barracks. We did not exactly know what was to become of us. Kent being our regimental station, we expected to be ordered to march and join the left wing in that county, but were still kept at Plymouth, where we met with great kindness and attention from the inhabitants in general, who are upon the whole, I think, an excellent and a moral people. We also fared sumptuously here, every description of food being both cheap and good. Fish in particular is most abundant and excellent. In short, we were here as comfortably and as well quartered as we could desire, and everything tended to make us perfectly satisfied with our lot.

We relaxed by attending the theatre occasionally, which is one of the best provincial ones in the kingdom, and at this time could boast some very good actors. There were a variety of other amusements, such as fishing, &c., which of course we indulged in occasionally. From hence I was called up to London to meet our Colonel, the Hon. Sir W. Stewart, to arrange our battalion concerns, &c, for the few latter years of hurry and confusion, and which was at last got done to the satisfaction of all concerned. Here also we began to replenish our wardrobes, which, it will easily be imagined, were not the most magnificent in the world on our first arrival.

But we were not long permitted the enjoyment of English society or English comforts, for we had scarcely been a month at Plymouth till we received an order to prepare again for foreign service, and the nature of that service being kept a profound secret, we scarcely knew what necessary articles of equipment to prepare. The general opinion, however, was, that our destination was some part of America, consequently we endeavoured to meet all contingencies by preparing both for a warm and cold climate. All hands of course were vigorously set to work, in order to be ready when the summons arrived, which we knew might be very soon expected.

An alteration was made in the arrangement of our battalion. The staff was ordered to proceed to join the other wing at Thorncliffe, which of course included myself, but Major Mitchell, who was now appointed to the command of these five companies, was anxious to take me out with him in the capacity of acting paymaster, and to his friendly and earnest endeavours, added to the kindness of Captain James Travers, who had at first intended to apply for that situation himself, but renounced it on my account, I am indebted for again having an addition of 10s. *per diem* made to my regimental pay during the continuance of service on this expedition.

At length the order arrived for our embarkation, and on the 18th September, just two months from the day of our arrival in England, our five companies were sent on board His Majesty's ships *Fox* and *Dover*, both frigates of the smaller class, and which had been prepared for the reception of troops, by having a part of their guns taken out, and being, as it is termed, armed *"en flute."* The commanding-officer, with the staff and three companies, were put on board the *Fox*.

We laid in an immense sea stock of provisions, &c. not knowing how long we might be on the water, but unfortunately for us we had scarcely put foot on board, when the order was given to weigh and proceed to sea forthwith, so that no time was given for the stowing away of all the stock, which had cost us about *L.*24 per person; the consequence was, a great part of it was lost or destroyed, from its being knocked about the deck in the midst of the confusion and bustle consequent on the crew and the soldiers (strangers to each other) being set to work to weigh anchor and make sail in such a hurry. Little assistance was afforded us from the ship on this occasion. We thus lost nearly the half of what we had been at so much pains to provide; but such things being common occurrences in a life like ours, it was therefore vain to fret.

The force that embarked at the same time with us, consisted of the 93rd Highlanders, a company of artillery, some rocketeers, a squadron of the 14th Light Dragoons, without horses, and our five companies, the whole under the command of General Keane. The good people of Plymouth, as is customary, cheered us as we left their shore, wishing us the most ample success and good fortune, and which we, who had for so long a time been in the habit of conquering, did not for a moment admit a doubt of being fully realized.

We sailed, as I said, on the 18th September, and stood down the channel with a pretty fair breeze, till we reached what are commonly called its "chops," where we encountered adverse winds, and blowing a succession of gales (equinoctial, I imagine) which detained us beating off and on for seven days. This was as uncomfortable a beginning of our service as could well be imagined. High winds, with rain, and contrary to the way we wished them, were certainly rather trying to the patience of us landsmen, and there was something in our situation on board this ship which did not at all tend to alleviate our discomfort. In fact, we wished our fortune had placed us on board a transport rather than where we now found ourselves.

All the discipline and strictness of a regular man-of-war was enforced, without any of the countervailing comforts and conveniences usually found on board such ships; and to such a length was this carried, that because our officers sometimes stood on the quarter-deck, holding on, in the rolling of the ship, by the hand-ropes which surround the companion, not only these, but the ropes which were stretched to prevent people falling out at the gangway, were ordered to be removed, that nothing should remain by which lubbers like us might hold on in the heavy rolls to which the vessel was subject in gales like those I have been describing.

We were no less than twenty-four people in the cabin, twelve of our officers and twelve gentlemen of the commissariat department, so that we were sufficiently crowded, besides being in several other respects ill provided. But all this would have been borne with cheerfulness and good-will, had we not experienced such a total want of kindness and urbanity from a quarter where we least expected it, and from which that unkindness could be made most effectual.

We lost the fleet during the continuance of these gales, but sealed orders having apprized our commander where to rendezvous, we made sail for the Island of Madeira, which we reached on the 9th October, and where we found the fleet. Some of the wags of our other two companies on board the Dover, pretending to think we must have been cast away and lost, had erased all our names from the army list as defunct. This rather annoyed some of our folks, but it might have been easily seen it was only a little waggery in which they had been indulging themselves.

A day or two before we reached Madeira, we fell in with a strange sail, to which we gave chase, and brought her to; she proved to be an English merchant brig. It was said our commander wished to have a little independent cruise, which caused him to part from the fleet, and that there was a famed American privateer called the *Wasp* that had made a great number of captures, and which he was anxious to fall in with that he might take her. Had such a thing occurred as the *Wasp* appearing in sight, and we had given her chase, I could have compared it to nothing but to a vulgar simile which I have sometimes heard used, that of a cow endeavouring to catch a hare, for indeed she was, I believe, one of the fastest sailers that had ever been known, while we, on the contrary, were in comparison just like the cow to the hare.

This also must have been a piece of waggery on the part of those who first set such a report afloat, for no man in his senses would have ever thought of chasing privateers with the *Fox* frigate at the time of which I am now writing. I regret I did not go on shore on this beautiful island, the town and scenery of which were most inviting, but as our stay was only to be so very short, it was scarcely worthwhile.

We sailed again on the 11th, alter having first got a cask of excellent Madeira wine from the house of Messrs Gordon and Co. This was the best, I think, I ever drank. We stood almost due south, passing pretty close to Tenerife and the other Canary Isles, until we fell in with the trade-winds, when we kept more away towards the south-west. Our voyage now became delightful, for a gentle and refreshing, but constant and steady breeze, carried us on at the rate of about five or six knots an hour, without having occasion hardly to alter a sail or rope. We passed to the tropic of Capricorn on the 15th October, when our sailors prepared to indulge in the same innocent but amusing ceremonies that are adopted on crossing the equator.

Neptune, with his Amphitrite, got dressed in full costume, and every other appendage being ready, it only now remained that the commander's sanction should be obtained to their commencing the imposing ceremony; but no! his godship was dismissed in no very courteous manner, and told to go and attend to his duty. Thus the fiat of a greater than Neptune, even in his own element, reduced him from the godlike rank he held to that of a more forecastle sailor; and thus were all our expectations frustrated. In all the other ships of the fleet the amusement was carried on with the greatest good humour, as we could plainly perceive with our glasses.

On the 18th, we passed pretty near the Isle of St Antonio, the westernmost of the Cape Verde Isles, and then bearing off still rather more to the west, we kept our course generally at about 12 or 13 north latitude, and in this manner crossed the Atlantic.

From the time that we had entered between the tropics, we had seen numerous shoals of flying fish, some of which, when closely pursued, (by the dolphin generally,) actually fell on board our ship. A very accurate drawing of one of these was made by one of our lieutenants, a friend of mine, who, I believe, has it to this day. They were generally about the size of a herring, and much resembling that fish in shape and colour, with two fins projecting from behind their gills, nearly as long as their body. These are their wings, with which they can fly generally for 100, or 150, or sometimes 200 yards, when they fall again into the water. We also caught a dolphin about this time, our carpenter having harpooned it from the bow of the ship; but I was considerably disappointed in finding it did not exceed from twenty-four to thirty inches in length; and the hues of it, though beautiful when dying, by no means answered my expectations.

On the —— November, we made the island of Barbadoes, and anchored in Carlisle Bay, off Bridgetown, the capital of the island. It is not easy to describe the effect which is produced on an European the first time he beholds the beauties of a tropical country, and which, I think, he does in the greatest perfection while they are yet distant from him. Robertson's description of Columbus's first view of a West India island is, I think, as correct and as beautiful as anything can possibly be; and his feelings for the moment (heightened indeed by the circumstance of his having at length attained to his long-looked-for Western India) will describe pretty nearly what everyone must feel, who has not before beheld the productions of a tropical climate.

But oh! how is the scene changed when you get on shore! Nature indeed is still beautiful and rich beyond the conception of a northern native; but man—how fallen! Here (I think I shall not far err if I say) you behold man in his lowest state: the savages of the woods are, in my opinion, much higher in the scale of being than those whom our cursed cupidity has introduced to all our vices, without one alleviating virtue to counterbalance the evil. But how could the poor Africans learn anything that is good from those who do not practise good themselves?

One of our people while here said, "he thought the men were all rogues, and the women all unfaithful." Of the slave population the latter is certainly a correct description, almost universally, in Bridgetown; for, with shame be it spoken, their masters and mistresses calculate upon their worth as if they were brood-mares, by the number and the description of wretched beings which they can bring into this world of misery. What indeed could you expect from those who can thus act, and those who sanction such conduct, but the like treatment that Mr Shrewsbury met with, if you endeavour to show them to themselves or to others in a true light? While the strong man armed keepeth his castle, his goods are in peace; but let another endeavour to bind this strong man, and take his goods from him, and oh, what a resistance may not be expected!

Let the West Indians have slaves whom they may treat as cattle for their own gain and profit, even if it be at the expense of the souls of the poor wretches whom they thus destroy; but endeavour to show these degraded human beings that they are capable of being raised to a level with their unfeeling and avaricious masters, and you may shortly expect the fate of a Smith or a Shrewsbury, so regardless are these dealers in human flesh of their duty as men who must soon render an account of all their actions.

It may be said, that I saw little, while here, but the very worst of society, and this may in a great measure be true; but it is evident that such things were done and sanctioned at Bridgetown when I was there, in 1814, as led me to pray that my lot might never be cast among such people.

I now gladly turn from this scene of vice and misery, and pursue my narrative.

In the bay at this place a hulk was stationed for the reception of prisoners of war. Our boats usually passed pretty near it on going on shore for water. A number of Americans were on board as prisoners. On one occasion, or more, I believe, they called out to our fellows as they passed under her stern, "So you have come out from England to attack our country, have you? I hope you have brought your coffins with you, for you will need them before you return." And, in truth, many of those fine fellows to whom this insolently coarse but patriotic speech was addressed, did indeed require coffins before the business we were going upon was finished.

We left Barbadoes on the ——, and, passing down through the midst of the islands, we left St Lucia on our left and Martinico on our right hand. We also passed close to Dominico and Guadaloupe, with several smaller islands which I do not recollect, and, keeping to the southward, passed St Christophers, Santa Cruz, Porto Rico, and St Domingo, having a fine view of the whole as we moved delightfully along. This latter large island took us more than two days in passing; but on the 21st we came in sight of Jamaica, the chief of our West India possessions.

We stood off and on near to Port-Royal till the 23rd, when we made sail to the westward, and on the 25th came to anchor in Negril Bay, at the extreme west end of the island of Jamaica.

Here we found several sail both of men-of-war and transports, having on board the troops which had been engaged in the operations against Washington and Baltimore, &c., and consisting of the 4th, 21st, 44th, and 85th Regiments, with some artillery. They were not strong indeed, having been considerably reduced by their late arduous services; but their numbers, added to ours, we thought quite sufficient to enable us to make a descent upon the American coast near New Orleans, which it was now whispered was our destination: indeed this had been conjectured from the time we left England, but nothing certain was known, and even now it was not officially made public.

A day or two after our arrival here, two of the West India regiments also joined us, the 1st and 5th, at least a part of both; so that we now mustered a respectable force. Admiral Sir Alexander Cochran commanded the naval part of the expedition, be being here on our arrival on board the *Tonnant* 84; several smaller vessels also, with stores, &c. &c. joined us from Port-Royal. When the whole were collected together, we felt proud of our fine force, which we vainly imagined nothing we should have to encounter could withstand for a moment: but the battle is not always to the strong; and we were shortly after painfully reminded of this truth. But I must not anticipate,—evil always comes early enough.

During our stay here, I went on shore for a few hours, and visited some of the farms or plantations. Indeed, while we remained, the place where we landed was generally like a fair; for the inhabitants bad assembled in great numbers, bringing with them live stock and poultry and vegetables, &c. for sale, all of which were greedily bought up at prices high enough, I warrant you. the vegetation at this place was most luxuriant, even in this the middle of winter almost; but I apprehend this was the finest season of the year, for it was not at all intolerably hot, and everything had the appearance which our country assumes in the height of summer.

An accident occurred whilst we continued here, which had nigh proved serious. The *Alceste* frigate, one day, in shifting her berth, run with her head right on board the Dover, where our other two companies were on board. She cut her up from the stern into the cabins, not less I am sure at the top than ten feet. Two of our people were in the cabin at the time playing at backgammon, and were not a little astonished to see the prow of another large vessel tearing its way right into the very place where they were sitting.

On the 29th, signal was made to weigh, when the whole got under way, and started in fine style; our now gallant fleet covering the ocean for many miles. We kept along on the south side of Cuba, and on the 3rd December made Cape St Antonio, the westernmost point of that large island. From hence we now stood to the northward, crossing right athwart the Gulf of Mexico. During our stay at Barbadoes, we had purchased a live sheep and a pig, as we feared our stock might run out before we landed. The sheep was productive of great amusement to our messmates, at the expense of the poor caterer. In all hot climates, I believe, the wool of the sheep becomes in course of time more like the hair of a goat than what it really is.

This was the case in the present instance, most of our people declaring they would not eat of such an animal, which was, as they conjectured, a sort of mule bred between a sheep and a goat; while the poor caterer was like to have the sheep thrown on his hand. This produced many a bickering, even after it was known that such was the case in warm climates; for they kept up the fun as long as possible, always trying to keep the unfortunate caterer in hot water about it. The sheep was killed, and produced excellent mutton—not fat indeed, but eatable.

We were not so fortunate, however, with our pig; it appears it must have been diseased—what, I believe, is usually termed measly. It was dressed without this being known, and eaten; and the consequence was, all the twenty-four of our mess, except myself and another were literally poisoned. In the middle of the night, when it began to take effect, the most distressing scene took place imaginable, and the medical men were kept busily employed for a considerable time afterwards preparing and administering emetics, which providentially had the desired effect on all, for in a short time the whole recovered; but had medical assistance not been promptly administered, the chances are some of them would have suffered. Its effects were something like *cholera morbus*, working both up and down in the most violent manner.

On the 10th December we made the American coast off Mobile, where we fell in with a vessel, on board of which was Colonel Nichols of the marines, with three or four Indian chiefs of the Creek nation, to which people he had been for some time previously attached, they being then at war with the Americans, and consequently our allies. They came on board our ship, and were shown everything curious; but their reason for visiting us was, that they might see our rifles, for they considered themselves good shots, and wished to examine our arms, with which they did not express themselves over-satisfied, as they had been accustomed to see no other description of rifles than those used by the Americans, which are both much longer and heavier, but carry a much smaller ball. Indeed they had never seen any military rifles, but only such as the above, and which are constructed solely for the purpose of killing deer and other game.

The gallant colonel endeavoured to amuse us a little on this occasion with the wonderful feats of his protégés. He told us, that they being generally very short of balls, were always very careful how they expended them in hunting; and that their rule was never to fire at a deer, until it was in the act of passing between them and a tree, that, should the ball go through its body, as it sometimes did, it might lodge in the tree on the other aide, and they would then go and pick it out, and recast it. We thought he ought to have told that story to his own corps the marines; for I believe he did not get many of us to give implicit credit to so wonderful a tale.

They were most grotesque-looking figures; most of them

were dressed in some old red coats, which they had got hold of by some means, with cocked hats of the old fashion. These I believe had been given them by some of our people, for they were English manufacture. But they had tremendous large rings, &c. hung in their ears, the laps of which were stretched nearly to their shoulders; some of them also wore rings in their noses; and some of them were without any sort of lower garments, having nothing but a sort of cloth tied round their waist, which passed through between their legs and fastened before. These people it was intended should bring their warriors to join us near New Orleans; but, owing to some cause with which I am not acquainted, none but these three or four chiefs ever came near us.

On the 11th we anchored near the Chandeleur Islands, at the entrance into Lake Ponchartrain. But it was discovered that the Americans had some gun-vessels, which, on account of their drawing only little water, had been stationed in this lake for its protection, and on our appearance had retired nearer to New Orleans. It was necessary that these should be previously disposed of in some manner, before the disembarkation of the troops could with safety be effected. None of our ships could follow them on account of the shoalness of the lake. An order was therefore issued for all the men-of-war to prepare their boats for an attack on these vessels, the chief command of which was given to Captain Lockyer of the Sophia gun-brig.

On the morning of the ——, they therefore assembled for this purpose, and pushed up the lake in search of the gun-vessels, which were discovered moored near some islands called by the natives, "Les Isles Malheureuse," or the "Unfortunate Islands," and which form the entrance from Lake Ponchartrain into Lake Borgne, or Blind Lake. No time was lost in attacking this formidable flotilla, consisting of vessels carrying from five to six guns each, and commanded by a lieutenant of the American navy, named by them Commodore Jones. A most determined and gallant resistance was made by the Americans; but superior numbers, with equal, if not superior courage and seamanship, prevailed, and in a short space of time the whole were captured.

Both the commandants were severely wounded, with a great number of officers and men killed and wounded. Nothing could exceed the gallant intrepidity, I understand, with which our boats advanced to the attack; for, from experience I am well convinced, the fire from those gun-vessels must have been most destructive; for better shots, either with artillery or small arms, do not exist than the Americans.

Orders were now issued for the army to prepare to land; but the distance, from where we had been obliged from shoal water to stop to the town, being so great, it was determined to form a sort of depot on a small island, near the mouth of the Pearl River, called Pine Island; and further to facilitate the transport of the troops, small brigs, &c, were sent as far up the lake as possible, into which the troops were put successively from the larger vessels, and from which they generally took their departure, for the above island.

On the 15th our people left the *Fox*, and were moved up the lake into one of the brigs before noticed, where we were packed in as tight as herrings, there being near 400 men on board a little thing scarcely calculated to contain the fourth of that number, and where there was not literally room to lie down. But, on the 19th, we were relieved from this rather close confinement; and being put on board of long boats, we pushed off for the island, which lay at a considerable distance, notwithstanding the measures that had been adopted to shorten our voyage.

The weather proved extremely rough and unpleasant, which rendered our trip neither over-safe nor comfortable; and to mend the matter, the seamen on board our boat were rather in the wind, and did not manage her so well as was desirable; for, poor fellows, they had been engaged in this fatiguing service for several days, (a considerable number of the troops having been previously landed,) and were consequently the more easily prevailed upon to indulge when grog came in their way. Our middy too was quite worn out with fatigue, and slept nearly all

42

the time we were on board. Our boat was several times on the point of being swamped, for the water came in quite plentifully on occasions of her being laid down by sudden squalls. Another boat, which accompanied us, had her mast carried away.

We landed on the island before mentioned in the evening, and of course looked out for the best shelter we could find. But it was a complete desert; nothing but reeds grew on it, except a few stunted and scrubby bushes at the lower end of it. It came on a most severe frost during the night, which I understand caused the death of several of the sailors, who had indulged perhaps a little too freely, and had lain down without any covering.

Some of the poor blacks also, I understand, suffered in consequence of the severe cold, a thing with which they were totally unacquainted, and against which they were ill provided, having nothing but their light and thin West India dress to keep it out. It was laughable the next morning to see them examining so intently the ice which had been formed on the pools near our bivouac. They could not conjecture what it was; some of them asserting it was salt; while the greater part were totally at a loss respecting it. I had by great good luck got into a sort of hut belonging to some of the officers who had previously landed; but I do not remember in all my campaigning to have suffered more from cold than I did this night, and was extremely glad when daylight appeared, that I might be able to move about.

Proceed to Attack the Enemy

By the 21st, the whole army had been landed on this island, when they were told off into brigades, and inspected by the general. During our stay here, about five or six French Americans, (the natives of New Orleans, or neighbourhood,) arrived as friends, and told us that there were scarcely any troops in the district; so that we had nothing to do but to land on the opposite side, and march right on to the town, and that the inhabitants would welcome us most cordially, and that no resistance might be expected. I did not, I confess, put much confidence in their information, and believed at the time, that they came more as spies than with any view of befriending, as they pretended, our cause.

More correct information was obtained from Spanish fishermen, who had been following their occupation at the mouth of a creek on the New Orleans side of the lake, and who had come across, I believe, at the suggestion of Major Peddle, our assistant quartermaster-general, who had been despatched to find out a suitable landing-place for the army. From one of them, I learned afterwards that there were troops in the town, commanded by General Jackson, and that a battery of two guns had been erected on the road, by which we must advance. What they told the General, I do not know, but fancy he saw no reason to alter his plans, from the information of either party.

Everything being ready by the morning of the 22nd, the advance guard, commanded by Colonel Thornton, and consisting of the 85th and 95th Regiments, with two light three-pounders, some artillery and some rocketeers, accompanied by a few artificers to repair bridges, &c. embarked on board the boats, that had been assembled for the purpose—two companies of the 93rd followed us; these troops occupying the whole of the boats that could be mustered in the fleet, consequently the remainder of the army had to remain where they were till the return of the boats. The distance was not less, I should think, than from thirty to forty miles.

We pushed off about two o'clock p.m., the wind being favourable for a considerable part of the way, but it failing, the men were obliged to commence with the oars. We were completely wedged in, so that there was no moving, let the call be ever so urgent. I suffered much from a severe pain in my side, from being obliged to remain so long in the same position; but we endeavoured to divert the tedium in the best manner we could by amusing stories, &c. My luck placed me on board the *Bang-Up*, a fine cutter belonging to the admiral, and commanded by a countryman of mine, a Lieutenant Foster of that ship. We did not reach the mouth of the creek, or *bayou*, as it is called by the natives, till a long time after dark.

As we approached it, some light boats were sent forward with Captain Travers of ours and his company, to endeavour to surprise a regiment of the enemy, which we knew were stationed in some huts at the mouth of the creek, and which huts belonged to the Spanish fishermen before mentioned. From the information they gave, the best arrangements possible were made for effecting this; for Travers, moving silently on, and landing his men at the opposite ends of the hamlet, there remained no way of escape open for the troops in the houses.

As soon as all was ready, they rushed forward and secured the whole picquet without a single shot being fired, with the exception of two men, who preferred venturing into the marsh, in rear of the huts, where it is not improbable they perished. The duty was conducted so quietly, and so expeditiously, that very few of the other troops knew anything of the matter; but this alone secured us a landing without opposition, for had a firing been begun on either side, it must have alarmed the American army, who, no doubt, would have used their endeavours to oppose our landing.

We soon after began to enter the creek, but such was the darkness of the night, and the shoalness of the water, and such the uncertainty of the way by which we had to proceed, that very little progress was made during the remainder of the night; daylight, however, enabled us to move forward at a brisker pace, but from the obstacles that had presented themselves in the dark, the squadron of boats was sadly dispersed; and when we reached the head of the creek, only two or three of the light boats, with the staff and naval officers, had arrived, and considerable intervals of time elapsed between the arrival of the different boats with troops; so that had the enemy been aware of our intention, and had they had a force of a few hundred men hid in the high reeds which grow in this marsh, they might, I am persuaded, have cut us off in detail, for from the causes before mentioned, no two boats were sufficiently near to assist each other.

We got on shore about an hour after daylight; and right glad was I to be enabled to stretch my legs, which had been kept motionless for the last sixteen hours. As soon as the whole advance-guard had landed, and a few planks had been thrown over a deep rill which we had to cross, we moved forward towards the high ground, Captain Travers' company leading; and, in order to magnify the appearance of our force, should any concealed American be looking on, we extended our files to double the usual distance, and thus passed through a wood which skirted the swamp, and which it was necessary to traverse before we could reach the open country, which we did about six miles below New Orleans.

As soon as our advance cleared this wood, they observed a good-looking farm onstead, towards which they moved in double quick time, and arrived just in time to seize and, make prisoner a Monsieur Villerey, a major of the militia, just then setting off to join his people. We heard (but I will not vouch for the truth of the report) that a considerable body of the enemy had been assembled on the highroad, near to Monsieur Villerey's house, but on learning that we had landed, and were moving rapidly forward, they separated, one part retiring towards the town, while the other went down the river.

Our advance now moved on with celerity, and dashing on to the different farmhouses in the neighbourhood, seized several groups of arms at each of them, which it seems had either been abandoned by the troops to whom they belonged, or had been collected there for some military purpose. They captured at some of these farmhouses to the amount of twelve or twenty stand; and in all not less than fifty.

Monsieur Villerey unfortunately contrived to make his escape, through the too great leniency of one of our lieutenants. I think the most probable opinion respecting the arms and the troops assembled near Monsieur Villerey's is, that it was the militia of the district just at that moment assembling, which will not only account for the arms being found in such numbers, (under the verandas of the houses,) but also for Monsieur Villerey himself being then on the point of setting out in his warlike costume, and the number of men which were observed near his house.

About twenty militiamen were also captured in and about these houses. Except there, the whites had all abandoned their houses; but a considerable number of black slaves remained at each, whether of their own accord, or left to protect the property, and occasionally convey information to their masters, I know not. As soon as our advance had sufficiently reconnoitred the adjacent houses, &c. the whole of the troops moved on past the house of Monsieur Villerey, and turning to the right, followed the great road to New Orleans for about half a mile, till a suitable piece of ground presenting itself in the neighbourhood of some other farmhouses, the whole turned in to a green field a short distance from the road, and forming into close columns of battalions, commenced bivouacking for the night.

The road ran partly on, and partly alongside of the river dike. Immediately between the troops and the river, this dike was perhaps about three feet high. On our right was a farmhouse, and a little to the right and front another—the latter a pretty large one—all these, and indeed all the farmhouses in this neighbourhood, are surrounded at one end by the huts of the slaves, and generally on the other by barns and other outbuildings, and in the rear a garden or orchard. The ground in all this country, which is perfectly flat, apparently of alluvial formation, is divided into fields, &c. by wooden paling of the common description, very few hedges being to be seen.

The situation in which the troops were placed, was as follows, *viz.* The artillery and rocketeers in one line; immediately behind them, my battalion and the 85th, in close column; the 4th in rear of us, and the 93rd two companies in rear of the 4th; the whole in close columns. The men, as soon as dismissed, instantly set about cooking, for they had had nothing from the morning before, and it was now considerably past mid-day. Captain Travers' company, which had formed the advance-guard, still remained in front as a picquet, and occupied a post on the great road, about a mile in front of the division.

About three o clock p.m., we were all alarmed by some shots at the advanced picquet; and, on enquiry, found that an American staff-officer, escorted by about thirty cavalry, had come galloping down, no doubt for the purpose of reconnoitring us; when within distance, our people instantly fired, one of which shots wounded the staff-officer, and another killed a horse, but they contrived to get him off. This caused the whole of the troops to fall in till the cause of alarm was ascertained, after which they set about their cooking again with great glee.

Considerable discussion now began to take place amongst the knowing ones, as to the merits and demerits of our situation, in point of security; and of course various opinions were given on the occasion. One officer of ours, a particular friend of mine, did not hesitate roundly to assert, that we were in a most unprotected and dangerous situation. I do not remember exactly the reasons he assigned; but certainly, could he have foreseen what yet remained in the womb of time, he would have had much stronger reasons for his opinion.

Another company of ours, (Captain Hallen's,) and one of the 85th, were ordered to prepare at dusk to relieve the picquet in advance; and as I messed with Captain Hallen's company, I accompanied it on this duty. I did not go with the main body of the company, there being no house at that post, but with one section, commanded by Lieutenant Forbes, and we occupied a small house to the right, and a little to the rear of Captain Hallen's party, which was stationed on the great road. The company of the 85th occupied the large farmhouse before-mentioned, a little to the right and front of the column. I had purchased an excellent turkey on our arrival at Monsieur Villerey's house, which we had dressed at this little house, and made a most hearty meal indeed, after which we took each a tot or horn of grog to comfort us.

We had not long finished our comfortable meal, when we were astounded by the report of heavy ordnance, apparently dose to the bivouac of the column, and which reports followed each other in quick succession. A cheer was also given, but by whom, or what the occasion of the firing was, we were totally at a loss to conjecture. I at first imagined it was some of our men-of-war that had been able to pass the forts down the river, and that they were firing a salute and cheering in consequence; and yet this seemed a strange conjecture; but we did not long remain in suspense, for we were soon after informed of the real state of the case, that it was a large American schooner, with at least fourteen guns, and which she had been enabled to bring to bear upon our unfortunate bivouac with the most deadly precision, great numbers having fallen at her first broadside.

The troops of course dispersed in some measure, leaving their fires, which had too well served as a direction for the fire of this terrible schooner. But the time was not far distant when we should have other enemies to encounter; for by the time the schooner had fired a dozen broadsides, a noise was heard in our front; and just at this moment an American was brought in by a man from Captain Hallen's post, who had foolishly come right into the centre of his picquet, and asking if they could tell him which way the regulars had gone. This showed that he was a young soldier, who did not know our troops from his own; but it also showed that the regulars which he was seeking could not be far distant; consequently, everything was got ready to give them the best reception possible; but as the people we had heard in front of the post where I then was appeared to be rather to our right, I feared lest they might get unawares upon the company of the 85th, which was stationed in the farm behind us.

I consequently set off with all dispatch to give them timely warning, but when I arrived there, I could not find the officers, nor could I see where the picquet was posted; I therefore thought they must be on the alert at the bottom of the garden, which lay in the direction in which we heard the noise; and meeting here an officer and several of our men, who had moved in this direction, from the fire of the schooner, I told him I was certain that Hallen would be shortly most vigorously attacked, from the information I had learnt respecting the regulars, and advised him to collect all the men he could, and proceed forthwith to reinforce him at the advance. This he instantly did, and it was well, for by this time the firing had commenced in volleys at that post.

I then returned to the picquet-house, where I had previously dined, and found the officer was going round his sentries; but as the firing was going briskly on at Hallen's post, I expected every moment to be attacked here, and began, in the absence of the officer, to post the men as advantageously as the nature of the ground would admit.

The house stood on a little path, or bye-road, running across the country, from the river towards the wood, and which, before he could get into, the enemy would have to clamber over a railing which lay on the side from which they were advancing. On the hither side of the road was a ditch, with a hedge, almost the only one to be met with, and a little copse of small trees. Into this copse I put the men, extending them along the inside of the hedge, which would not only keep them from the view of the enemy, but be some little protection from their fire, and would leave them the more at liberty to retreat when overpowered by numbers, as it was certain they must shortly be.

But all my labour was in vain, for when Forbes came from visiting his sentries, he did not approve of my disposition, but took them all out, and formed them on the open road, without any cover, and with a hedge and ditch in their rear, both of which they would be compelled to pass the moment the enemy pressed upon him. I felt annoyed, not only at his want of courtesy to me, but that he would thus expose his men to almost certain destruction, without being able to effect anything against the enemy, or at all check his advance. I accordingly left him in a huff, and went again to try to find the picquet of the 85th in the house behind us.

I was determined to make a more close and thorough search than I had done before, and for this purpose went over the gates, &c. into the yard behind, when lo, I found myself within a yard or two of a strong body of the enemy, which had got into the garden at the lower end, and were just advancing to the house. I crouched down, and hid in the best manner I could, and luckily was enabled to creep off without their discovering who I was.

Just as I reached the outer gate, I found a sergeant of ours there, to whom I said, we must set off with all possible speed; and accordingly we both took to our heels, and ran like heroes; the noise of which brought the fire of twenty or thirty rifles after us, but luckily without effect.

I now made the best of my way towards where I judged the main body of our people were, on the great road, in order to inform Colonel Thornton of what I had seen, of this column of the enemy having got possession of the house and garden I had just left, and by doing which they had nearly separated the advance picquet from the main body. He said he had sent two companies of ours, and two of the 85th, to the house immediately in the rear of this I speak of, and in a short time afterwards they and the Americans came into close contact, for they immediately commenced firing; and where as strange a description of fighting took place as is perhaps on record.

The enemy soon discovered from some men, whom they had unfortunately taken, what the regiments were that were opposed to them—and with all that cunning which the Yankees are famed for, instantly turned it to the best account—for in several places they advanced in bodies, crying out at the same time, "Come on, my brave 85th!" or "My brave 95th!" and thus induced several of our small detached parties to go over the rails to them, supposing they were some of our own people, when of course they were instantly made prisoners. This ruse did not always succeed, however, for some of the parties turning restive on their hands, refused to surrender, and thus a fight hand to hand took place, and in which they generally had the worst of it.

On one occasion of this kind our people made a body of them prisoners. The men and officers being requested to lay down their arms, the officer, after surrendering, when he saw there were not many of our people, drew a sort of dirk or knife, and made a stab at the officer of ours who had taken him. We instantly cried out to the men near him, one of whom took up his rifle and shot the villain through the body. They had before this time brought two of their regular battalions close in front

51

of our advance, which did not consist of more than 100 men, and were pouring in dreadful volleys into that small but gallant detachment; but even in this they showed themselves young soldiers, for they formed up the two battalions in line at about forty or fifty yards in distance from the post, and gave the words "ready—present—fire," with all the precision of a field-day; but being so near, of course every word was heard by our people, who, at the critical moment, always took care to cleave as close to the ground as possible, by which they escaped most of their shot.

They then up and at them, and, pouring in a desultory but most destructive fire, brought great numbers of them to the ground. Their force, however, was too great to be opposed successfully by such a handful of men, and these brave fellows were at length compelled to yield a little ground; but it was not more than just to enable them to cover themselves, and form again in proper order; and from this time all the efforts of these two battalions were unable to remove them. Indeed, not long after, our people became the assailants, and, advancing again, retook their original position. Poor Hallen was severely wounded on this occasion, and lost about forty of his men.

Two or three naval captains came also to see the fight at Hallen's post, one of whom soon fell severely wounded. The other, the gallant captain of the *Dover* frigate, with whom part of our people went out, and with whom we all came home, behaved most nobly. Whenever the enemy had fired their volley, he cried, "Now, my lads, up and give them another broadside!" and thus contributed, by his animating conduct, to inspire all around him with confidence.

Poor Forbes just met the fate that I expected. He stood upon the road, and opened his fire upon the enemy as they approached; but they being perhaps more than twenty times his number, he was instantly compelled to give way, after being himself wounded, having his sergeant killed, and losing nearly the half of his men. The schooner all this time kept up a most galling and incessant fire. Some attempts were made with our light three-pounders, and with rockets, and even with small-arms, to compel her to sheer off, but they were all in vain. Her men, protected by her stout bulwarks which surrounded them, defied all our efforts, and continued to pour in both round and grape wherever they judged, from the direction of the fire, our people were stationed. Luckily the darkness of the night rendered her fire less destructive than it would otherwise have been.

A considerable body of the enemy had penetrated to the house immediately on the right of our original bivouac, where the firing was kept up between them and the parties opposed to them with great spirit for a long time; but the general, having detached the 4th regiment to form line a little to the rear and right of that house, completely secured that flank from being farther turned. Notwithstanding this, the skirmishers of both armies extended to the wood, some of whom we found lying the next morning almost touching each other. The firing now began to slacken, the enemy having been repulsed at all points, and, towards three o'clock in the morning, it had completely ceased, when they retired, leaving us in possession of the warmly-contested field.

My battalion had been extremely unfortunate in this action; for almost at the very outset, when the attack on Hallen's picquet commenced, Major Mitchell, our commandant, had taken a party of about twenty or thirty men, and advanced for the purpose of supporting that post. Between the bivouac, however, and the point he intended to reach, he unexpectedly fell in with a large body of Americans, (for it was so dark he could not distinguish who they were,) when both himself, and all the men he had with him, were made prisoners. The loss of our five companies in this action was about 120 men; that of the 85th more, I believe; and in all, I think, it amounted to about 300 men. The loss of the enemy must have been considerably greater, if we are to judge from the number of dead they left on the field, and, which is a good criterion, the general average being about ten wounded for one killed.

Nothing could equal the bravery of the few troops we had

in the field on this occasion. Their numbers certainly did not amount to 1800 men; while the enemy could not have had fewer than from 4000 to 5000. They had two regular regiments, the 7th and 44th; they had a large corps of irregular riflemen from Kentucky, and another stronger corps from Tennessee, with all the militia of New Orleans and its neighbourhood, every man who is able being compelled to bear arms in case of invasion. They had about 300 irregular horse, whether militia or not I cannot tell, but think it likely they were in all at least 4000 men—with the great and effectual assistance of the schooner, which did us more mischief than 1000 men could have done, probably not so much by the loss she occasioned us, as, by being able to fire on our flank, and even in our rear, she rendered the enemy the most essential service, besides the fire of the ship on our advanced picquet.

We were thus completely surrounded on three sides, and had not the troops behaved with the most determined courage and intrepidity, we must have been driven back, and eventually the greater part would have been taken prisoners; for the path to the water was quite narrow, and even should we reach the head of the creek where we landed, the boats had probably all left it by this time to return for the other troops. Indeed it was reported afterwards, that the arrangements of General Jackson were such, that we were to have been attacked in the rear at the same time as in front, and by the schooner; but the troops for that purpose either not being in readiness, or being too distant to arrive in time, were too late to take part in the action, but arrived about three o'clock in the morning, when they met with a half-drunk artillery-driver of ours near Mons. Villerey's house, as he was returning from the field,, and who, seeing a large body of men, which he took for some of our other regiments that had landed, cried out to them, "Come on, my lads, for the Yankees never got such a licking in their lives!" This, it is said, had the effect of frightening them back, without proceeding farther.

I will not vouch for this being fact, but such was the report the next morning; and indeed it is feasible, from the number of people (apparently going with orders, &c.) which we saw galloping down on the other side of the river in the afternoon; and it is certain that a considerable body of militia must have resided down the river, setting aside the report which I mentioned, of some troops having retired in that direction in the morning, when we first advanced; and nothing would have tended more to our complete overthrow than such an attack on our rear, could it have been accomplished.

I might here mention, that Captain Hallen saw the schooner as she passed his picquet, on her way down from New Orleans, on which he instantly despatched a man with the information; but she having the current in her favour, sailed much quicker than the man could run, consequently his information came too late.

I omitted to mention also, that a large ship of 20 guns came down the river at the same time with the schooner, but being less manageable than that vessel, she had anchored abreast of Hallen's picquet; and that he had to sustain her fire, as well as that of the troops in his front, during the whole of the attack of the 23rd. She remained at that spot without moving.

I will here also notice another circumstance which took place at this post. An American rifleman fell into the hands of some of Captain Hallen's people, who, when he was brought in, were desired to take his arms from him. These he seemed reluctant to part with, and said to the officer, "Recollect I shall hold you responsible for that rifle, if you take it from me!"—on which the officer took hold of it by the muzzle, and flung it right into the river. I daresay the poor fellow thought they were a strange sort of people he had got amongst; and I doubt not he had set a great value upon his rifle.

Another officer and myself had a providential escape the next morning, for we had scarcely left a little wooden hut, behind which we had taken up our abode, and slept for a few hours after the fight, when bang comes an eighteen-pound shot right through the house, just at the very spot where we had a minute or two before been sitting. It seems the captain of the schooner, which still lay abreast of us at about 800 yards distance, and from which this shot had been fired, was determined we should not occupy any of the houses in the vicinity, for, beginning with our hut, which was nearest to him, he fired into every house within reach of his guns, although he saw as plainly as we did that most of them were filled with the wounded; nay, he carried his savage cruelty so far, that he actually fired on a party of the 85th as they were removing one of their wounded officers.

It could not be pleaded that he did not know what it was, for, being only half-a-mile distant, and much elevated above our level, with a glass he could see as well as we could what they were doing, for they were carrying the poor fellow on a bier, on their shoulders. He continued this cruel work all the next day, the ship also giving us an occasional shot. One shot which he fired went through the front of a house in which some of our wounded men were lying, and, striking low, it carried the knap-sack out from under the head of a man of ours named Rayour, which he had put for a pillow, without doing him the smallest injury. I could not credit the story till I went and actually saw the hole by which it entered, the knapsack and the shot lying near the fireplace.

After this I went to view the house where I had fallen in with the column of the enemy the night before, and where the 85th were now stationed; but the fire of the schooner still con-tinued, one shot from which we saw was directed towards us. It fell right in among the 85th, and, striking a corporal about the breach, as he was endeavouring to get out of its way, it passed out at his breast, on which he gave himself a sort of shake, and fell lifeless to the earth.

Nothing could exceed the great annoyance this mischievous schooner continued to be to us all that and the next day, for they not only saw everything we did, but we could not move in any number without being saluted with an 18 lb. shot, and we had no means of retaliation. But during the 25th, efforts were made to get up some heavier guns from the fleet, and everything hav-ing been settled as to the plan, &c., a battery was constructed as close to the water's edge as possible in the river dike, and a number of gun barrels having been collected from those broken, &c. during the late fight, a sort of furnace was erected for the purpose of heating shot, with which it was determined to give her a salute the next morning.

Everything succeeded admirably. The battery was constructed, embrasures cut, and shot heated, and all ready by daylight on the morning of the 26th; of course we were all looking out to witness the effect, and most noble it was, for when the guns opened out upon her, the people on board seemed quite thunder-struck, and although they attempted to return our fire, it was only like the blows of a man beat blind by his antagonist, for her shot fell in every other direction but that in which she should have thrown them. However, they could not stand to fire more than one round, as our hot shot rendered their situation very soon untenable, and taking to their boats, they made their escape to the opposite shore with all expedition.

The distance from the battery to the schooner had been so accurately measured by Major Blanchard, who superintended the construction of the work, that almost every shot and shell penetrated the hull of the vessel, and in a short time after her crew had left her, she broke out into a blaze of fire, which soon reaching the magazine, she blew up with a loud explosion, to the great comfort and joy of all our army. This of course deserved and obtained three as hearty cheers as I believe were ever given by Britons, and no doubt the Americans were greatly chagrined at the loss of their fine and exceedingly useful vessel.

A shell or two were directed towards the ship, but she having seen the fate of the schooner, got out her boats, which, taking her in tow, she set off up the river in all haste. Could a battery have been constructed to fire upon her at the same time, it would have saved us some hard knocks afterwards. She, however, effected her escape, and we now remained in peace for a few days at least.

On the 25th, Sir Edward Packenham and General Gibbs had arrived; the former immediately assumed the command, and they both set off to the front to reconnoitre the enemy and the kind of country around us. Every night since our arrival the enemy had been incessant in their means to harass and annoy us, as in truth they had a right to do if they pleased, but it was exceedingly distressing to the troops, and therefore I mention it. They seldom let an hour pass during the night, that they were not firing at some of our out sentries, and on some occasions they brought the body of irregular cavalry, before mentioned, immediately in front of our outposts, and fired volleys, which, although it did not do much injury to our advanced picquets, had the effect of turning out the whole line, and that often repeated, with the annoyance from the schooner, certainly did not leave us much time for comfortable rest.

They frequently lay in ambush for the reliefs of our sentries also, and patrols, and fired upon them sometimes with effect. In short, they did all they could to annoy, and weary us out, but of which we ought not to complain, as they were defending their own country, and allowances ought to be made in such a case that would not be tolerated in an army having no interest in the soil. I trust Englishmen will be equally zealous and bitter to their enemies should our country ever be invaded.

Preparations For a Grand Attack

The remainder of the army all arrived during the 24th, and were put in bivouac in an oblique direction, with their front to the late field of action, their right thrown back towards the wood, and their left towards Mons. Villerey's house. The 93rd formed line in advance at an angle of the wood, as a sort of outpost, while the 85th and ours were stationed in and around the house, to which I have so often alluded, *i.e.* where I fell in with the column of the enemy. Our advanced picquets remained the same as before the action. If I might here be permitted to hazard an opinion, I should say that had we advanced upon New Orleans the morning after the fight, I think there is little doubt we should have been successful; for when an irregular and undisciplined body of troops once meet with a reverse, it is difficult to bring them into action again with that steadiness and determination which they often evince in their first essay.

I understood General Jackson had some trouble in keeping them together after their defeat on the night, of the 23rd, and the only mode in which he could get them to form was, in planting the first who retired in line near the road, and as each successive detachment arrived from the fight, they were made to form on their left, the whole line sitting or laying down for the remainder of the night. It is easy to perceive that they would have been quite unmanageable should they have been seriously attacked, while their spirits were depressed by their recent failure, and as the works which we afterwards encountered did not then exist, at least only in part, I think they would have retired after a very slight resistance indeed. I had the information as to the manner in which they formed, from some of those who were made prisoners, and who witnessed it. All this, however, is merely the opinion of a private individual, who judged from appearances only, and it is not in the nature of things probable that I should be able to form so correct a one as those who possessed more ample information.

After the arrival of the two general officers before mentioned, the army was told off into brigades as follows, *viz*. the 1st brigade, commanded by General Gibbs, consisted of the 4th, 21st, and 44th British, and 5th West India regiments; the 2nd brigade, commanded by General Keane, consisted of the 85th, 93rd, and 95th British, and 1st West India Regiments, (observe, the West India regiments had by this time become exceedingly reduced in point of numbers from cold and hardship, which they seemed unable to bear, and very soon after almost ceased to be regiments, so many of them were sent away sick;) the artillery was commanded by Colonel Dickson, an excellent officer; the squadron of the 14th Light Dragoons not being able to get mounted, formed the guards at the hospitals, and at headquarters, &c.

Everything having been previously arranged on the morning of the 28th, we advanced in two columns, the right near the wood commanded by General Gibbs, and ours on the left by the great road near the river, commanded by General Keane. The enemy had all along kept possession of those farmhouses which lay at some distance in front of our picquets. They were consequently driven from these as we moved forward, which we did, I should imagine, to the distance of about three miles, their picquets retiring gradually before us. We here discovered that the enemy had thrown up a strong fieldwork, which extended from the river to the wood, and which consequently shut up every avenue to our farther advance, without fighting.

We also found that their numbers had considerably increased, as we could perceive by the immense bodies of troops behind their works. As we pressed upon their picquets as they retired, we got a shot or two at them with our field-guns; but everything remained quiet within their lines till we had arrived within about 400 yards of them, when they opened out on the head of our columns as destructive a fire of artillery as I ever witnessed. One shot struck in the column of the 85th, which knocked down two officers and about ten men. My battalion was leading, and being partly extended skirmishing, they did not offer so fair a mark for artillery as a solid body, and consequently escaped this.

The ship also, which was anchored a little in advance of their work, opened her broadside on the columns on the road at the same time. Our gun and howitzer, the only two pieces we had there, endeavoured to return the fire of the ship, but without doing her much injury. When the fire was found to be so galling, the troops were moved off the road into the fields on the right, and my battalion advancing about 100 paces farther, was ordered to lay down in a sort of ditch which was there, and to shelter themselves the best way they could.

The 85th and 93rd formed also more to the right, and secured themselves as well as the nature of the ground would admit. It was only intended as a reconnoissance, consequently the troops did not advance farther, as soon as the nature of their position was ascertained. It appeared to be a high dike of casks, formed as a breastwork, with a considerable quantity of artillery mounted on it, and with a sort of canal or wet ditch in front of it.

Of course, all this took some time to ascertain, daring which they kept up an incessant cannonade, both from their works and from the ship. The latter poured in an immense quantity of large grape, which rendered the situation of those exposed to it extremely unpleasant. Our two field-pieces were very soon silenced by the superior fire of the enemy, and in an hour after our arrival at this point, there was not a man left with them but the officer, who was quite a youth, but yet stood as steady as if he had been on a common parade, although all his men were knocked down about him. I never witnessed more devoted heroism than this fine young man displayed. One shot, nearly towards the last, struck off his sergeant's head, and sent his cap spinning over a ditch, where another officer and I had taken up our post.

Some rockets were also tried from this point, both against the ship and the enemy's works, but those directed against the vessel flew quite wide of the mark, and totally failed. Some of those fired into the works, we saw pass over the heads of the men posted, in them, but whether they produced any effect we could not see.

The enemy either had set fire to the houses near us before they retired from them, or they had fired heated shot with a view of producing that effect; but we had not been long here ere the whole of the houses in the neighbourhood were in one grand and terrific blaze of fire. I do not exactly know what was done on the right, for we could not see distinctly for some trees which grew in the garden of the farm in that direction, but imagine they encountered something similar to ourselves, as the play of artillery from the enemy's line in front of them was equally unceasing with that in our front. Not a man showed himself out of the enemy's works.

When everything was ascertained that could be, the troops began gradually to draw off, but this was obliged to be conducted in a very cautious manner, or the loss from their fire would have been severe. The 93rd retired first, by separate wings, afterwards the 85th, but ours (reference to 'ours' means 95th Rifles) did not leave their ground till after dark, when, I believe, some of the Yankees began to advance in a rather triumphant and bullying manner, but were taught to keep at a respectful distance by a few shots well laid in among them. A party of sailors had been sent forward to bring off the two field-pieces, there being no artillerymen left to do it, and we had no horses. They undertook and accomplished this task most cheerfully and effectually, without a man hurt I believe.

The loss of my battalion on this occasion was not great. The army now took up a fresh position in which to bivouac, at about a mile and a half distance from the enemy's line, but which they could easily reach with the shot and shells of their larger pieces. The headquarters were removed from Monsieur Villerey's house to a large farm or *château* behind our new lines, and which were formed in the following manner, *viz*.:—the 4th and 44th composed one line, with their right near the wood. The 21st formed on their left, but with an intervening space between them. The 85th and 93rd formed one line on the left of the 21st, with an interval between their line and that regiment. This latter line was rather in an oblique direction, with its front towards a farmhouse in advance and to the left, and where my battalion was ordered to take its station.

This latter post was more exposed to the enemy's shot than any of the others; it being a good deal advanced, and being close to the river, the guns from the opposite shore ceased not firing on it, generally with hot shot. The men were put into a sugar house belonging to this *château*, the floor of which being sunk a little below the surface of the adjoining earth, protected them wonderfully; but on occasions they had their very cooking utensils knocked off the fire by the enemy's shot, in consequence of the exposed situation of this house.

The acting quartermaster and myself being deemed civilians, and having no inclination to be deprived of our natural rest at night, as long as we could be allowed to obtain it, took up our abode in one of the outhouses at headquarters, which we found unoccupied, and where our respective duties could be carried on with as much facility as if we were in the same house with the battalion, the distance between them being only about half a mile.

Here, also, the sick and wounded were brought, where they could enjoy more comfort than in the sugar-house, till an opportunity offered of sending them down to the shipping. To secure our front a little more, and to protect the troops against the shot from the opposite shore, a redoubt was thrown up about half a mile in front of the right, and pretty near the wood; while batteries and breastworks were constructed on the road, to fire on any vessels of the enemy which might come down the river. These latter were principally constructed of hogsheads of sugar, which were found in the sugar-houses of the different plantations in the neighbourhood. But nothing could have answered worse than they did for this purpose, the enemy's shot going quite through them, without being at all deadened almost by the resistance they offered.

In front of the left also, inside the road, a breastwork was thrown up, which secured the persons of a corps of marines and sailors, who occupied that part of the line. This body was, soon after the 28th, landed from the fleet; and the latter, having brought small arms on shore with them, acted as a small battalion.

It is evident the enemy must have worked incessantly, from our first landing, to complete the work they occupied; for, from the information I before mentioned, as given me by one of the Spanish fishermen, it is clear they had only two guns, mounted on something like a battery, on the great road. But now that work extended even into the wood, a distance of at least three quarters of a mile, and at this time there could not be less than ten or twelve pieces of heavy-ordnance mounted on it. We were told by the slaves who had remained in the houses, that the ditch behind which they had constructed this work was a sort of small canal, which the gentleman who owned the property used for the purpose of transporting the produce of his farm from thence into the river. From this time we could plainly perceive great numbers of men continually at work upon it, mostly blacks, of which they would, of course, have abundance; but their white people also (the army, we conclude) were constantly employed upon it. We could see distinctly that they were widening and deepening the canal in front of the work, and raising the parapet to a considerable height.

It was now determined to try what our heavy ship-artillery would do against this work. Accordingly, the greater part of the army were employed in bringing up these unwieldy machines, and to effect which required no slight power and perseverance, as we had no means of transport but the sheer strength of a number of men combined, to drag them successively through the deep soil. A sufficient number of them having been brought up by the 31st, strong working parties were employed all night in erecting two batteries, as near to the enemy's works as they could with safety venture, and getting the guns, carriages, and ammunition, &c., into them. These were formed principally of casks, &c., filled with earth; and I am not sure that some sugar hogsheads were not used on the occasion. However, at daylight on the morning of the 1st Jan. 1815, the whole of the troops were ordered under arms, and moved forward to nearly the same points they occupied on the 28th *ult*.

This morning there was an extremely thick fog, which greatly favoured our movements, the Americans being, I believe, totally ignorant that any alteration had taken place in the situation of our army. As soon as the fog cleared away, our artillery opened out a tremendous and thundering cannonade upon the enemy's line, which so completely astonished them, that there was not a shot returned for twenty minutes at least, so little did they expect heavy artillery there. Nay, we heard afterwards that a great number of the irregular troops were so alarmed, that they actually quitted the lines without orders, and were posting off to New Orleans, and were with great difficulty brought back again.

As soon as they perceived, however, that nothing more than a cannonade was intended, and that our troops did not advance to the attack, they commenced gradually with their artillery against ours, the fire of which increasing as their confidence increased, they were not long in silencing our guns, and in dismounting some of them. The fact is, our works had been thrown up in such haste, that they were not nearly so strong as they ought to have been made, had there been more time; the consequence was, their shot penetrated into every part of our works, and caused us not only considerable loss in artillerymen, (with one officer killed,) but, as I said before, actually dismounted a great many of our guns.

This consequently entirely failed of having the desired effect; but with such a very favourable opportunity as this morning's fog presented, together with the alarm and terror with which the enemy were struck on opening our artillery upon them, there is not the most distant doubt that we should have at once got possession of their lines, had we but advanced to the attack. It is true, we were not prepared for passing the ditch, having no fascines or other necessaries for that purpose; but the resistance, in my opinion, would have been so slight, that we might almost have chosen our own place to cross it; and it was not very deep at any place. The battalion of sailors were quite annoyed at being kept looking on, while so fair an opportunity, as they thought, offered, and were crying out one to another, "Why don't we go on? what is keeping us back?"

'Tis not to be doubted that the first effect of any new thing in warfare is always the most certain of producing success, particularly against inexperienced troops; but let them see and know the whole of the effects that such a thing is calculated to produce, and the alarm wears off, and confidence and courage return with wonderful rapidity. So it was here; the first fire of our guns struck them dumb with amazement and terror—But mark the contrast! Both the latter part of this day, and on the 8th, at the general attack, how little they seemed to care for all the artillery we could bring against them!

Their gun, a 32-pounder, was a most bitter antagonist to our principal battery. This happened to be erected nearly in front of that part of the line where this gun was situated, and when it fired, its shot always struck the battery at the first bound, and then it ricocheted into the redoubt where I had taken up my post. General Keane, with a part of his brigade, was in this latter work, and some of them narrowly escaped the effects of the numerous balls thrown from this gun. We were told the captain of the schooner, after having been deprived of his vessel, bad been appointed to the charge and management of this gun, with some of his crew to work it; and indeed it seemed very like the bitter and determined manner of our former opponent, for any of the other guns seemed like children's play to the unceasing and destructive fire of this heavy piece of ordnance. I could distinctly see that they were sailors that worked it—one of whom, a large *mulatto*, with a red shirt, always spunging her out after firing.

In what I am going to relate, I know I shall incur the risk of being deemed a *traveller* by some of my readers, but that shall not deter me from telling what I plainly and repeatedly saw with my own eyes, assisted by a glass. At the distance of three quarters of a mile, I could distinctly perceive the ball from this gun every time it was fired, it appearing like a small black spot in the midst of the column of white smoke, and which gradually grew larger in appearance as it approached us. In many instances I was providentially the cause of saving some of the men who were in the redoubt with us, because, seeing which way the ball was coming, I told them when to lie down; and on one occasion was the shave so close, that it actually carried away one of the men's packs as he lay on the ground. Another shot struck about three feet above our heads, and carried away part of a piece of timber which supported a shed just behind us.

I forgot to mention, that, after the 28th, the Americans, conceiving that the guns of the ship would be of more use if taken out and placed in batteries, this was accordingly done; the greater part of them being planted on the other side of the river, and being completely on our flank, were enabled to annoy our people considerably, who were posted near the great road.

About two or three o'clock in the afternoon of the 1st, the army began again to retire to its bivouac, leaving covering parties to protect the batteries; and after night, the whole having formed, working parties were sent to bring off as many of the heavy guns as possible. Some of these, however, they were obliged to bury in the earth, not being able to drag them away before daylight next morning. This work seemed more oppressive and fatiguing to the troops than the bringing of them up did, inasmuch as they were animated in the latter instance by the hope of their being able to effect something against the enemy through their toil and labour; but now disappointment added poignancy to their sufferings.

However, although things began to assume not quite so favourable an aspect as formerly, yet everything was borne with the greatest good-will, as they were still confident of all their laborious services being ultimately crowned with success. In all these fatiguing services, the sailors bore an ample share, and were of the very utmost benefit to the whole army, for they could readily contrive the means of moving those immense masses of metal by purchases, &c., which to a soldier would be utterly impossible. Indeed, throughout the whole service, the gallant tars deserved the very highest praise, for they were equally brave as laborious and willing.

All hands, both soldiers and sailors, had been up the whole of the night of the 31st, and now up again all night of the 1st. This was very trying, no doubt. If anything like dissatisfaction was evinced, this incessant toil and want of rest in encountering it, arose more from a desire to be led on to the attack, than from any wish to be rid of their labours, however painful these were. As this attempt had failed, no other scheme now appeared to present itself, but a vigorous and well sustained attack on their line; for several efforts had been made to penetrate through the wood, to endeavour to ascertain whether it was possible to turn their position at that point, but all these efforts had failed.

The last that was attempted was conducted by Lieutenant Wright of the engineers, but both himself and nearly all his party perished; for it seems they fell in with a body of American riflemen, who, being much better accustomed to travelling in woods than our people were, fell on them, and, as said before, nearly cut off the whole party; yet it is evident it was not utterly impassable, or the two parties could not have met.

I do not recollect to what regiment the men belonged who accompanied Wright, but think it probable they were altogether unacquainted with that description of service, which led them into the fatal snare in which they fell. I am confident I saw blacks, who passed and repassed by the wood, but it is certain that no attempt upon a large scale could be made in that direction to turn their position; and it was probably the better plan to abandon the idea altogether.

A very excellent expedient was however devised, for the purpose of turning the right flank of the enemy; it was certainly a bold and vigorous idea, and one which, if successful, would no doubt have secured to us the victory and the possession of New Orleans. This was no less than cutting a canal, in order to unite the Mississippi with the lake by which we had arrived, and by getting boats out of the latter into the river, to transport a sufficient number of men to the opposite shore, for the purpose of making a diversion in aid of the principal attack on this side.

Nothing could exceed the grandness of the conception. Accordingly, all hands were set to work to widen and deepen the rill of water which flows into the creek at the landing-place, and, continuing it up past Monsieur Villerey's house, to let it enter the river a little above that point. This, as may easily be conceived, was most laborious and dirty work; and, lest the health and spirits of the troops should suffer from such incessant fatigue, they were told off into four watches or spells, each of which followed the other in regular succession, so that the work never stood still. When it had reached near the house and high-road, screens were put up on the latter, to prevent the enemy on the opposite bank of the river from seeing what was carrying on; but as

C A N A D A

Quebec

Montreal

Kingston

York

Niagara

Osego

Albany

Ft.Duquesne

PENNSYLVANIA

Germantown

Philadelphia

Baltimore

WASHINGTON

VIRGINIA

Guilford

N. CAROLINA

Cowpens

Camden

S.CAROLINA

Eutaw

GEORGIA

Savannah

Charleston

Pensacola

Orleans

FLORIDA

HAVANA

CUBA

SAN DOMINGO

Jamaica

NICARAGUA

Ft.Mackinaw

Crown Pt.

Ticonderoga

Saratoga

Bennington

Boston

Rhode I.

New York

Plymouth

Wilmington

Yorktown

Halifax

Louisbur

NOVA SCOTIA

Ft.Edward

Breton

MAINE

R.Richelieu

L.Champlain

L.George

Chesapeake Bay

R.Roanoke

Delaware R.

R.Ohio

Alleghany

Bahama Is.

S.Eustatius

Montserrat

St.Kitts

Nevis

Guadeloupe

Galanta

Dominica

Martinique

S.Lucia

Barbados

S.Vincent

Tobago

Trinidad

NORTH AMERICA
AND
WEST INDIES

0   250   500 MILES

Leeward
Is.

Windward
Is.

the blacks were passing and repassing almost continually by the wood, as I before mentioned, no doubt the Americans were well acquainted with what we were doing.

On the —— General Lambert arrived with the 7th and 43rd Regiments, to our great joy, two finer regiments not being in the service. Consequently every eye now sparkled with hope, that our labours and privations would soon terminate, as everyone confidently anticipated a favourable result, and seemed still inclined to despise that enemy who had shown us that we could not do so with impunity. We were glad to meet many of our old Peninsular friends in these two fine corps, and of course welcomed them to the New World in the best manner we were capable of. They took up their ground a little in front of the canal which was cutting, there not being room sufficient for them in the line of our bivouac. We were now about 7000 effective troops, and all beginning to cheer up again, imagined nothing could withstand us.

By the 6th the canal was finished, and the boats brought up into it. There was obliged to be a lock in it at the entrance from the river, for the strength of which Sir Edward, our chief, I understand, expressed his apprehensions, but was assured by the engineer that there was not the slightest danger. I give this merely as report.

On the 7th the arrangements for the attack next morning having been completed, orders were issued to that effect. The arrangements were as follows, *viz.*— a corps consisting of the 85th regiment, with 200 sailors and 400 marines, and the 5th West India Regiment, with four light fieldpieces, the whole under the command of Colonel Thornton, was to embark in boats by twelve o clock, and to be all across the river by daylight next morning. This force would amount to about 1200 or 1300 men, and were destined to attack and carry the works on the opposite bank, getting possession of the guns without allowing them to be spiked if possible, when they were to be turned upon the right flank of the enemy's position, on this side the river, to favour our attack.

It is clear, then, that this movement should precede that of the grand attack by a considerable space of time. In the grand attack the troops were to be disposed as follows, *viz.*—The right column, under General Gibbs, was to consist of the 4th, 21st, 44th, and three companies of my battalion (3rd-95th), which latter were to extend as close to the enemy's work as possible, previous to the advance of the column, and, by maintaining a constant fire, were to endeavour to keep the enemy down as much as possible. The 44th was to be divided; one-half of that corps was to carry fascines, &c., which they were to throw into the ditch on reaching it, in order that the remaining regiments of that column might be able to pass it. These fascines were to be had in the redoubt I before mentioned.

The other wing of the 44th was to lead that column, followed by the 21st, and then the 4th, Regiments. This was to be the principal attack. The left column, commanded by General Keane, was to be composed as follows, *viz.*—one company of the 7th, one of the 21st, one of the 43rd, and two of ours. The whole to be supported by the 93rd regiment. These were to make a feint attack upon the half-moon work which the enemy had constructed near the river, and if opportunity offered, to turn it into a real attack, and penetrate the enemy's line, co-operating with the other column.

Our two companies were to act here in the same manner as the other three with whom they were to form a junction, thus covering the whole front of the enemy's work. Some blacks of the 1st West India regiment were to enter the wood on the right of our right column, and to keep up as much noise as possible by firing and sounding bugles, &c. to induce a belief that a large body of troops was moving in that direction. The reserve, under General Lambert, was to consist of the 7th and 43rd regiments, and was to be so stationed as to be able to render aid to either of the attacking columns. Strict orders were given that no obstacle was to be permitted to retard the advance of the columns, but that they were to press forward and endeavour to overcome every hindrance that might present itself.

As far as I recollect, and from the information I have since gained, these were substantially the orders issued, and arrangements made, on this occasion. The commanding-officers and heads of departments were also assembled, and each told the part he had to perform; on which occasion, I understand, the commanding-officer of the 44th expressed himself in terms which I could scarcely conceive it possible could fall from the lips of a soldier, which were, that "it was a forlorn hope with the 44th."

In all my campaigning I never yet heard a commanding-officer who did not look upon the post of danger as the post of honour, and who did not rejoice, as if a favour was conferred on him, when appointed to an arduous or hazardous duty. Had the commanding-officer of the 44th served in the Peninsula under our illustrious leader there, he would, I am confident, have been animated by a quite different spirit. After dark I went with my commanding-officer and adjutant to view the ground over which our battalion was to march next morning, and to find out the wooden bridges, &c. over some ditches which lay in the way, that no delay might take place when they were to be called upon to act.

I was sadly disappointed at our not meeting with any other commanding-officers engaged in this most necessary duty, and at the time I expressed my apprehensions as to the result. I pointed out to him the different manner in which the business had been conducted previous to the assault of Badajos, and previous to the attack on the enemy's position on the Nivelle, where every commanding-officer, or others, who had any particular duty assigned to them in the next day's operations, were brought to ground from which it was clearly pointed out to them how they were to move and act; but here all seemed apathy and fatal security, arising from our too much despising our enemy.

This latter, I believe, was the principal cause of our not taking the necessary precautions, and consequently of our failure; particularly the commanding-officer of the 44th ought to have been brought and shown where the fascines were lodged, that no excuse of ignorance on that score might be pleaded. A rocket thrown up was to be the signal for the troops to advance to the attack, after they had been properly posted under the cover of night for that purpose. I own I did not at all feel satisfied with what I had seen and heard, and retired to rest with a considerable degree of despondency on my mind; and as I knew I could render little aid to the service in a case like the present, I determined I should not take any part in it, for I almost felt confident of its failure.

The whole of the troops were at their post by the time appointed; but, unfortunately, as the sailors, &c. were getting the boats out of the canal into the river, the lock gave way after only a very few had passed it. Thus the whole business seemed at one blow to be totally ruined. Every effort was mode to remedy the evil, but it was irremediable. They toiled, however, to get more boats into the river, but the delay had been so great that it began to draw towards dawn before they had effected anything worth mentioning. Poor Sir Edward seemed like one bereft of his reason, for this failure had blasted all his most sanguine hopes; and as the troops were now close under the enemy's works, and could not be withdrawn before daybreak, nor without being perceived by the enemy, he thought it as dangerous to turn back as to go forward with the operation, consequently he ordered the rocket to be fired, although it was considerably past the time for the attack to take place, and no troops on the opposite shore.

As soon as this was done, he galloped to the front. But the enemy had been quite prepared, and opened such a heavy fire upon the different columns, and upon our line of skirmishers, (which had been formed for some time within about 100 or 130 yards of the enemy's work,) as it is not easy to conceive. I was not in it as I said before, but I was no posted as to see it plainly. But the 44th, with the fascines, were not to be found. Their commanding-officer had taken them considerably past the redoubt where the fascines were placed, and when he bethought him of what he had to do, he and his men were obliged to turn back to seek them; and thus, when he ought to have been in front to throw them into the ditch to allow the other troops to pass over, he was nearly half a mile in rear seeking for them.

But I believe it would not have availed much had there been there in time, for the right column never reached the point to which it was directed; but from the dreadful fire of every kind poured into it, some of the battalions began to waver, to halt and fire, and at last one of them completely broke, and became disorganized. Sir Edward seeing this rushed forward with his hat in his hand, and endeavouring to animate them by his presence, he cheered them on to advance again; but at this moment he fell, after receiving two wounds, the last of which was mortal.

General Gibbs also fell nearly at the same time mortally wounded, and was borne off the field. Thus was the right and principal column deprived of both its leaders; and although one regiment gave ground, and could not be brought again to the attack, the other continued to keep in a body, although any attempt now must be hopeless, and they were losing such numbers of men that they must shortly be annihilated. They accordingly retired without effecting anything.

The left column succeeded somewhat better: but, as things turned out, it was only to enhance their own loss.

They forced their way into the circular work before mentioned, in which they made all the men who defended it prisoners. But the canal still lay between them and the main work, which was passed only by a plank; and being so few in numbers, it would have been madness in them to attempt to go beyond where they had at present stationed themselves. Indeed, they were in a most critical situation; for, being within a few yards of the enemy's main body, they could not move without being shot through the head by their riflemen; and it was not till they had threatened to shoot the prisoners they had taken, that they induced the Americans to desist from attacking them; for by this time General Keane also had fallen severely wounded, and the 93rd had been nearly cut to pieces; and General Lambert, with the reserve, had been obliged to advance and cover the retreat of the other columns.

Colonel Dale, who commanded the 93rd, fell early in the

action, and the command devolved on Colonel Creagh; this officer, being unwilling to retire his regiment without effecting the object aimed at, although the men were literally mown down by the murderous fire of the enemy, and the other column had given way, still endeavoured to advance, but was at length reluctantly compelled to retrograde, taking care to keep his men together. This showed a fine and noble feeling in him, and is equally honourable to his gallant regiment; but unfortunately it tended only to swell the list of killed and wounded on this lamentable occasion.

My people (the 95th) were thus left to shift for themselves, and to get away in the best manner they could. But being extended, and not being so good an object for the artillery to fire at as the columns, they escaped with much less loss than could well be supposed. Some few of them reached the ditch when they saw the columns advancing, and which they say could have been passed with ease; but the columns never advanced so far, which had they done, and that rapidly, their loss would not have been half so great; for the enemy's troops in front of the right column were evidently intimidated, and ceased firing for some seconds as the column approached; and there is little doubt, had they pushed on to the ditch with celerity, the Americans would have abandoned their line; at least, such is my humble opinion. But the poor fellows on the left, who had gained the only work which fell into our hands on this bank of the river, were still detained there, unable either to advance or retreat; and not one durst show his head above the parapet, or he was instantly shot dead.

Such was their confined and critical situation at this period, that an officer of the 7th, whose name I forget, being himself rather tall, and wearing at this time the high narrow-topped cap, could not squeeze in sufficiently close to cover himself completely by the parapet, the top of the high cap he wore sticking above the top of the work. This part of the cap, which was visible to the Americans within the line, had no less than four or five rifle-shots put through it while he lay there, but without touching his head. All this information respecting these three companies I had from Lieutenant Steele of the 43rd, one of the officers who was in the work.

They were obliged at last to adopt a very singular but politic expedient, which was, to make one of the American prisoners embrace a man of the 43rd, and thus to stand up together to see what was going forward; for hitherto they were totally ignorant, from the causes above assigned. The enemy durst not fire in such a case, for fear of killing their own man. The news they now learned was most disheartening indeed, which was, that the whole of the British had retired, and that the Americans were coming out of their lines, and were moving in the direction of that work.

Nothing now remained but to surrender, or to make an attempt to retreat, at the risk of being every man knocked down. The latter, however, they preferred; on which Colonel Rennie, of the 21st, who commanded these three companies, was the first to make the experiment, and in doing which, the moment after he left the fort, he fell to rise no more. They thought it better for them all to go at once, and instantly the whole party made a rush out of the work. The greater part of them providentially succeeded in effecting their escape, although many a brave fellow fell in the attempt.

An Attack Upon Mobile

It now remains to detail the operations of Colonel Thornton's party. It will be seen, that, although his people were all ready at the appointed hour, they could not get a sufficient number of boats to transport them to the opposite shore. In fact, they did not get on board till it was near daylight, and then only about one-half of the appointed number. But, although at the risk of sacrificing himself and the few men he took with him, he hesitated not to make the attempt of fulfilling his orders. The signal for the general attack, however, was made before he could reach the opposite bank, and he had then to land, and after making his disposition with the few troops he had, to advance and attack a corps of 2000 men, mostly covered by works, some of which were extremely strong.

He dashed on, however, the advance of the enemy giving way before him, till coming to their principal battery, he was obliged to detach a part of his force through the wood on his left to turn their flank, while he with the remainder attacked in front. This was conducted in such a soldierlike manner, that, after a short conflict, the enemy gave way on all sides, and retiring with precipitation, abandoned to the victors batteries and works containing sixteen guns of various calibre.

But, alas! all this success came too late; for the principal attack had by this time ended in a total failure, attended with the loss of three out of four generals, and with nearly 2000 officers and men killed, wounded, and made prisoners. Had Providence prospered the work of the canal, and the troops could have been got across at the appointed hour, and in sufficient numbers, there is every reason to believe that the effect produced on the main body by such a powerful diversion, would have tended to the complete overthrow of the whole force before us; for so insecure did General Jackson feel himself to be after our establishment on the other bank of the river, and so alarmed at its consequences, that, in the evening of the fatal day, he would not consent to a cessation of hostilities, to enable us to bring off our numerous wounded, till General Lambert (who had now succeeded to the command) agreed as a preliminary to withdraw the force under Colonel Thornton from that bank; and this, although with great reluctance, the General was compelled from motives of humanity and other causes to consent to.

Before, however, a final answer was returned to General Jackson, I believe it was suggested to our general, that, with the possession of the other bank of the river, and with the 7th and 43rd nearly yet entire, and with the remainders of the other regiments, our chances of success had not yet entirely departed, particularly as Jackson evinced such eagerness for our withdrawing from that bank. General Lambert in consequence used means to ascertain the feelings of the troops on this proposition, but with-

PLAN OF NEW ORLEANS

out their knowledge of his having done so; but I regret to state, they seemed utterly hopeless of ever being able to overcome such formidable difficulties as had presented themselves, particularly now that their means of overcoming them had been so lamentably diminished. The idea was consequently abandoned.

In this negotiation between the generals, which continued for some hours, Lieutenant-colonel Smith, our assistant adjutant-general, had repeatedly to pass from army to army with flags of truce, before the matter could be finally arranged. This officer was most indefatigable in his exertions on this unfortunate expedition, and to him the army is greatly indebted for his zeal, ability, and gallantry, on this and every other occasion where they could be of service to his country, and by those in authority no doubt they are duly appreciated.

Thus terminated the fatal attack on the lines of New Orleans—a termination probably as disastrous in its consequences as any of modern date—not even excepting that of Buenos Ayres; for that, discreditable as it was to our arms, did not cost the lives of such a number of fine soldiers; and I fear we have not yet experienced the full consequences of this failure, for it is certain that the Americans are greatly elevated by it in their own estimation, and it is not improbable they may be thence induced to maintain a higher tone in all their future negotiations with this country.

One instance may be to the point, as showing the feeling of individuals of that country on this subject. A fellow in the shape of an officer asked Colonel Smith, (I think it was,) "Well, what do you think of we Yankees? Don't you think we could lick any of the troops of the continent easily?"

"I don't know that," says our officer.

"Why, I'll prove to you," says Jonathan, "that we have shown ourselves the best troops in the world. Didn't the French beat the troops of every other continental nation? Didn't you beat the French in the Peninsula? and haven't we beat you just now?"

This of course was conclusive, and no farther argument on that subject could be advanced.

The remainder of the troops retired in the evening to their sorrowful bivouac, worn out and sadly dispirited. All that night was of course devoted to bringing off the unfortunate wounded; but several of those who fell for in advance had been taken into the American lines, and, I have every reason to believe, were treated with the greatest humanity. Every effort was used, during the continuance of the truce, to bring away the great numbers who lay wounded in the different parts of the field; and on this as on all other occasions, the sailors with their officers, evinced the utmost solicitude to render assistance to the army; a great number of them were employed all night on this distressing duty.

During this whole of that afternoon, both while the negotiations were pending, and at other times, the American officers were unceasing in their endeavours to induce our soldiers to desert and join their army. Too many, I regret to say, listened to their offers, and accepted them. To some they promised promotion, to others money or grants of land; in short, they were more like recruiting sergeants, I understand, than the officers of a hostile army. My battalion did not quit the field till after dark, and it is from some of them I have this information.

A group of two sergeants and a private of ours were accosted by an American officer of artillery with a request that they would enter the service of the United States; that the sergeants should be promoted if they wished to serve, or that they should have grants of land if they preferred a civil life; but that, if they chose to enter the army, he would ensure them the rank of officers. Our people listened to this harangue for some time, and then began, I regret to say, to give him some bad language; telling him, at the same time, that they would rather be privates in the British army, than officers among such a set of raggamuffins as the Americans, and told him to sheer off or they would fire upon him.

This so exasperated the cowardly villain, that he went off instantly into the line, they watching him all the while, and pointing the gun, of which, it seems, he had charge, it was fired, and knocked down the private, who was only wounded, however, by the shot. Innumerable attempts of this nature were made both now and all the time we remained before their lines subsequently, but which attempts, I am proud to say, as far as I have been able to learn, failed in every instance in the men of my battalion.

Much about the same time, an American soldier came within about 150 yards of our line, and began to plunder such of the killed or wounded men as he thought possessed of anything valuable. He at length commenced upon a poor wounded man belonging to my battalion, which being perceived by a Corporal Scott of ours, he asked permission from his captain to take a shot at him. This being granted, (although a sort of truce had been established while the negotiations were going on,) he took up his rifle, and taking a steady aim, he fired, and tumbled the plundering villain right over the body of the poor wounded man.

The loss of our five companies in this attack amounted to seven officers and about men killed and wounded. Some of the other regiments, the 93rd in particular, had suffered dreadfully, having lost more than half their numbers. The sad ceremony of burying such of the officers whose bodies bad been recovered, together with attention to the wounded, occupied several days from this period, and sending the wounded, who were able to bear removal, to the shipping, kept great numbers of the remaining men continually employed; and the attention of all was now turned towards drawing off from this scene of our late disastrous attempt.

The general entered into a negotiation with Jackson about being permitted to send a portion of our wounded down the river in boats; for which permission some equivalent, which I forget, was to be granted on our part, and , which, after considerable discussion, was eventually agreed to. The sick, the wounded, the stores of every description, were now despatched as fast as circumstances would allow; but the effecting of this occupied not less than nine days, during the whole of which time the enemy was incessant in his attempts to harass and annoy us. All their heavy ordnance was brought to bear on our bivouac; the sugar-house our people occupied, and even the headquarters, did not escape; night and day they kept up a fire of shot and shells upon these points; but the distance being considerable, no very great mischief resulted from it, further than the continual state of uneasiness and alarm in which it kept the troops.

On one occasion, however, a shell was thrown into the lines of the 43rd, who had since the attack occupied a part of the general bivouac, and which, falling into a hut occupied by Lieutenant Darcy of that regiment, while he lay asleep, earned off both his legs as it fell. Poor fellow! he would thus be awakened in a rough manner indeed. I have since seen him in Dublin, the government having kindly compensated him by giving him a company, and I believe two pensions.

Several shells were thrown into the headquarters premises, but providentially without injuring any one. One fell in the yard while a party of troops was halted there for a short while, and which falling on one of the men's knapsacks, which he had put off, it carried it, with itself, not less than six feet deep into the earth. It did not explode. Some fell on the roof, which penetrated through all the stories to the very ground. Every night also the picquets were kept in a state of agitation and alarm by the continual attacks of small parties of our skulking enemy, and my battalion, as did the others also, lost considerable numbers by this petty warfare. In short, the men's lives began almost to be a burden to them.

There was another source of annoyance adopted on the part of the Americans on this occasion, but which, affecting only the mental, and not the bodily powers of our soldiers, was not so much heeded. Every day almost they assembled in large bodies on the parapet of their line, with flags of various descriptions, some with "sailors' rights" and numerous other devices, &c. painted on them, using the most insulting gesticulations towards those who were near enough to see them, a band playing Yankee Doodle, and other national airs, all the while, and sometimes ironically favouring us with Rule Britannia. Considerable numbers of our men deserted about this time.

Every encumbrance being removed, however, by the 17th, orders were issued for the march of the army on the following evening soon after dark, leaving the picquets as a rearguard, which were not to march till a short while before daylight. In retiring, some of the wounded, who were unable to bear removal, were necessarily left in the houses. where they had been collected; but there were not many so left, and no doubt the enemy acted humanely by them.

There were seven men of my battalion left, out of which three rejoined us after the conclusion of peace; the other four, I believe, were very badly wounded, and died in consequence. It was also necessary to abandon such of the guns as remained in the advanced batteries, because, both from their weight and their being so near the enemy, they could not be brought off without exposing our intentions of retreating. Neither were these numerous, and most of them only iron ship-guns, which are of no great value.

The movement commenced according to the preconcerted plan, and being conducted with secrecy and regularity, every soldier was brought off, over a country almost impassable, and where, if followed and harassed by an enterprising enemy, great numbers must have either fallen into their hands or perished in the swamp. But I believe, had the Americans even been aware of our intention, they would have hesitated before they came into collision with our highly exasperated army, and would scarcely have dared to attack us in the open field: they had had enough of that work on the 23rd, to give them a specimen of what British soldiers could do when met fairly, front to front.

The marsh, it may be necessary to mention, extended from the lower skirt of the wood to the fishermen's huts at the mouth of the creek. This creek we had sailed up on our advance, but this could not possibly be the case at present, both on account of our numbers being much too great for the number of boats, and of the danger to which it would have exposed the troops had they been attacked from the shore, but principally on the former account; a sort of road had therefore been constructed by our artificers, by cutting down boughs from the wood, and laying them across such places as required something on the surface on which to tread. This road extended, as nigh as I can judge, about eight or ten miles, and in passing which numerous slips were made into the sloughs on each side; but there being plenty of assistance generally at hand, they helped each other out: some men, I understand, were lost, however, in this night-march through the swamp.

Having arrived at the huts before-mentioned, the whole army set about forming such places of shelter as the desert swamp afforded. There were certainly reeds in abundance, but we wanted some sort of timbers for the support of die outward covering. We, however, did the best we could; and now every exertion was made by the navy to bring the army off from this most uncomfortable place of abode, and regiment after regiment were despatched as fast as the boats and other small craft could go and return, the distance from hence to the shipping being about seventy miles. While we remained here, we who were fond of shooting found plenty of wild-ducks on which to exercise our sporting abilities; but, alas I we wanted shot, and were therefore seldom able to bring home a couple for dinner.

A considerable number of slaves, belonging to the estates where we had lately been stationed, followed us down thus far, some of whom would not return, but were afterwards sent on board of ship. These, male and female, often amused us with their native dances, the men generally having a number of rings or bells about them, which sounded as they kept time to the tune. Some of their dances were, however, far from decent, particularly on the part of the females, which, it may be supposed, highly delighted some of our young and thoughtless country-men. Some were induced to return to their masters: for those who came on board of ship, I believe it was not till very lately that the two governments came to terms as to the remuneration which their owners claimed for them.

At length the turn came for my battalion to go on board, which we did on the 25th of January, when our whole five companies were put on board the Dover, the ship that had brought out two companies of the battalion, and which were then not much fewer in number than the five at present were; in fact, we had lost more than half. The whole army did not get embarked till ——, when the 7th Fusiliers came on board. This regiment had been necessarily left alone at the fishermen's huts till the boats could return, as before stated, to bring them off, and yet even this single battalion the enemy, with upwards of 10,000 men, dared not come down and attack, although there were no works to protect it in this exposed situation.

Nothing could possibly demonstrate more fully and clearly, that, notwithstanding the repulse they had unfortunately given our troops, they dreaded them in the open country; or else it must be attributed to the prudent sagacity of their leader, who, having gained a victory which he had previously scarce dared to hope for, now wisely resolved not to risk the tarnishing of his dear-bought laurels. It is not an easy matter to reconcile this cautious and timid conduct with their furious onset on the night of the 23rd, and with their boasting speeches after our failure on the 8th instant.

Now, while we remain at rest for a short while on board of ship, let us take a retrospective glance at the late events. It is certain we were singularly unfortunate. Providence, which had smiled upon us in our late operations against the most formidable army in the world, the French, here taught us most painfully, that the victory is not always to be gained by strength or courage. Indeed it was but a just punishment for the contempt we entertained for our opponents, and which unfortunate feeling, I believe, was almost universal. I own I entertained it in a high degree; for I judged it next to a moral impossibility that an army of undisciplined and unmanageable peasants, however numerous, could for a moment withstand the attack of those troops who had overthrown the victorious legions of Bonaparte.

But every soldier was a patriot, and they fought for their country, and for a country of all others most suitable for the operations of such troops; full of fastnesses, composed of creeks, and necks, and woods, &c. of all which they did not fail to take the utmost advantage. For this work of theirs, constructed on a spot of ground said to have been pointed out by General Moreau, completely shut us out from all approach towards the town, and compensated for every disadvantage under which they, as irregulars, laboured; for it was not only a formidable barrier to our army, but it gave them, by the protection it afforded their persons, all the steadiness of troops inured to combat, and permitted them the full exercise of that superior skill as marksmen for which they are famed, and which exposure in the open field would have deprived them of; for here they were covered up to the chin, and suffered comparatively nothing from all our fire.

But I fear we have something for which to blame ourselves on this occasion. It is certain, I believe, that they had been timely apprised of the destination of our expedition,, however secret we pretended to keep it ourselves, and if rumour may in such a case be permitted to go for anything, it is said that information was conveyed from Jamaica to New Orleans direct by a French ship, which left the former for the latter place sometime before our arrival. How she came into the possession of that information, I cannot justly tell. It is certain, however, that the Americans must have had timely notice, or General Jackson could not have had the men from Kentucky and Tennessee to oppose us the first night we landed.

I before hazarded an opinion, that had we pushed forward on the 24th December, we should in all probability have proved successful. I will say nothing as to the point of debarkation being well or ill chosen, although many have said we should have been more likely to succeed had we attacked Fort ———, which, after carrying, would have allowed us to land behind the town, instead of three leagues below it. These things I am totally incapable of judging of, from my ignorance of the country. I also before expressed my opinion, that had we attacked on New Year's Day, when our artillery produced such an effect on the appalled Americans, we should have had a better chance of carrying their works.

Another thing in which I venture to differ from the plan adopted by our lamented commander, is, that I would have employed the 7th and 43rd to the post of honour, instead of keeping them in reserve. They, it was well known, had each established a reputation for being the finest regiments in the service, and every reliance might have been placed in their executing whatever task was assigned them, if executable by human powers. Far different was it with those who unfortunately led the attack, for except one of the regiments of the attacking column, they had not any of them been conspicuous as fighting regiments.

It was, I believe, a well known maxim of Bonaparte's, always to put his best troops in front; if they were successful, their example served to stimulate the others to copy their example; if unsuccessful, their discipline and valour never permitted them to become so totally disorganized as to render the reverse irretrievable. The onset also of these better troops, must produce a for different effect on the enemy than the hesitating and dispirited attack of inferior ones. Had our troops on this occasion rushed forward to the ditch in double quick time, or at least at a quick march, I venture to affirm the work would have been carried with the fourth part of the loss of what they suffered.

Reason itself must point out to any man, whether acquainted with military matters or not, that to move slowly under a galling fire is more trying and destructive to the troops so moving, than to rush at once to the point aimed at; but much more, to halt at the very point where every firearm can be brought to bear upon them with the deadliest effect, is of all other modes of proceeding the least likely to succeed. They were thus exposed for hours to as destructive a fire as ever was poured upon the heads of an attacking army, while, had they pushed on at the rate I mention, a few minutes would have sufficed to put them from under the fire of the artillery at least, for when close to the ditch, it could not be brought to bear upon them.

Mark the mode in which the three companies on the left effected the task assigned to them. Before the enemy were aware almost that they were to be attacked, these troops were in possession of the work they were destined to storm; so quickly indeed that the defenders of that work had not time to effect their retreat, and were, as before noticed, made prisoners by the attacking party. This not only secured their safety while left there by themselves, but enabled them, in some degree, to effect their retreat with less loss than they would otherwise have been exposed to.

I have dwelt perhaps too long on this, but of all other causes I deem this to have been the greatest of our sad failure. It is lamentable, however, to be obliged to confess, that ill conduct on the part of some parties, but of one individual in particular, contributed in no small degree to our repulse on this melancholy occasion. For the rest, nothing could exceed the determined courage and patient endurance of hardship that the army in general evinced, and certainly nothing could exceed the gallantry of our leaders.

It was now determined to make an attempt upon Mobile, a town lying about thirty or forty leagues to the eastward of New Orleans. Accordingly, the fleet got under weigh and proceeded in the direction of the entrance into Mobile Bay, which is protected on the west side by shoals and Isle Dauphine, and on the east by a fort, built on a point of land called Mobile Point, and mounting about twenty pieces of heavy ordnance. Its name is Fort Boyer, I believe. Before our arrival in this country, an attempt had been made on this fort by one of our frigates, but which entirely failed, owing to her taking the ground on the shoals before mentioned. As she could not be got off, and as she lay under the fire of the fort, her crew were compelled to abandon her, but, I believe, not till they had first set her on fire; her wreck lay here when we came.

Until this fort was taken, no vessel of any size could enter the bay, consequently it became necessary to attack it in form. The brigade formerly General Gibbs's, consisting of the 4th, 21st, and 44th, was therefore landed a little behind the point, and proceeded without delay to invest it; the remainder of the troops were landed on Isle Dauphine.

We were put on shore on the 8th February, and instantly commenced hutting ourselves by brigades. Some of the officers had tents issued out to them; the acting quartermaster and myself had one between us. This island is almost covered with pine-wood, but in other respects it is nearly a desert, and without any inhabitants resident on it, save one family, a Mr Rooney, formerly from Belfast I understand, but now a naturalized American. He was married to a native of Louisiana, a lady of French extraction. He had been a midshipman in the American navy, but had been dismissed for some misconduct, it was said, and banished to this island. He appeared to us to be no great things.

I omitted to mention that the 40th Regiment had arrived from England before we left the banks of the Mississippi, but it being after the failure they were of no use, and were consequently not permitted to land. They were afterwards placed in our brigade, which now bivouacked near to the point of the island facing the bay. When we arrived, the island contained a considerable number of cattle, with pigs, &c. belonging to Rooney, but which had been permitted, as is customary in this country, to run wild in the woods, there being no danger of their leaving the island. These, however, soon fell a prey to such hungry fellows as we were, who had been for some time past on rather short commons. But they did not answer our expectations, being in taste, what may appear singular, quite fishy. This was attributed to their feeding so much on marine vegetables, there being little other pasture for them on the island.

A hoax was played off upon great numbers of our young hands respecting this fishiness. There was on one point of the island a considerable oyster-bed, and it was generally pretty near this that the cattle were found and shot, that being the most distant from our bivouac. It was therefore said the flesh of the cattle became of that peculiar flavour from feeding upon oysters. Some, without reflecting, credited this strange story, as the assertor generally said he had seen the cattle opening the oysters with their tongues.

This oyster-bed, however, was a source of great luxury to us, for it not only afforded us the means of rendering the salt junk more palatable by having an excellent sauce to make it go down, but it even afforded a most wholesome and delicious meal upon occasions by eating them raw. We also made the best use of our time when not employed on military affairs, in endeavouring to catch as many fish as we could; and for this purpose, my mess purchased from one of the poor Spanish fishermen before mentioned (and who, for the information and kindness they had shown us, were obliged to quit their habitations and follow us), an excellent casting-net, with which the acting quartermaster and myself occupied ourselves from day to day, generally bringing home a sufficient quantity of fish to serve our mess.

I never laboured more assiduously in any occupation than I did in this, not only from a relish for such amusement, but because we really wanted something to eke out our scanty meals. We at length got a seine-net from one of the men-of-war, with which we were not only able to supply ourselves most abundantly, but always had a large quantity to give away to the soldiers. Wild-fowl also were very plentiful when we first entered the island; but from the number killed, and the constant shooting at them, they soon became scarce and difficult to get at.

Here also there were abundance of alligators, and on our fishing and shooting excursions we frequently started them from their lurking-places, which were generally among the reeds by the side of an inland lake, or rather creek of the sea. On these occasions we seldom saw them, for they always endeavoured to avoid us; but wherever they ran along the bottom of the water, they stirred up the mud so greatly all the track they took, that we had no difficulty in tracing them. I never remember to have seen a live one on these occasions, but a dead one once afforded us considerable amusement.

One evening, on our return home from our constant occupation, there being three or four of us of the party, I was in front, and the acting quartermaster and the others in the rear of me. On a sudden I was alarmed by the cry of "Oh stop, here's an alligator!" and before I could look round, a shot was fired apparently into the earth, close beside their feet. I went back to see what was the matter, and found indeed, as he had said, an alligator, but one which I suppose had been dead for several months at least. It was buried in the sand, and only a part of its body appeared; but whether he imagined it might have placed itself in that situation intentionally, with the view of enticing its prey within its reach, or what other thought he had, I cannot tell, but, to make assurance doubly sure, he fired his rifle right into the body of the half-rotten alligator. He was long and often severely roasted about this afterwards.

A young one was caught alive, however, by some of the 14th Dragoons, and brought home to England, and afterwards, I understand, presented to the British Museum. All this while the siege of the fort was going forward, but as we had nothing to do with it, we had plenty of time, not only to hunt for extra prog, but to amuse ourselves in any other manner we pleased.

The army, about this time, was inspected by our chief, General Lambert, by battalions. My kind late commanding-officer. Captain Travers, who was severely wounded at the attack on the 8th, had rejoined by this time, although still very lame. During the inspection, the general said to him, "Travers, I am sorry to hear that your sergeant-major ran away on the night of the 23rd, during the attack."

"That is impossible, General," said Travers, "for he fought as bravely as any man could possibly do, and was carried off the field near the end of the fight, severely wounded. But I have a guess what has given rise to this report. A sergeant of ours left his battalion, I believe, either during or after the fight, and having taken up his quarters near one of the houses where the wounded were carried, the surgeon pressed him to remain with him as hospital-sergeant. I made efforts to have him sent to his battalion, but could not get it done. This must have been the cause of such a story having got abroad."

"Ah," says the general, "I am sorry that the poor sergeant-major should have lain under a stigma, of which he was altogether undeserving; and, now since we have done him an involuntary injustice, and he is a deserving man, we must try what amends we can make him for it." He accordingly recommended him for an ensigncy in one of the West India regiments; and before that day twelvemonth, he had risen to the rank of lieutenant. Nothing could be finer than the feeling of Sir John Lambert on this occasion; indeed, he has always shown himself a most excellent upright man, and a gallant officer.

About this time, a Russian vessel was detained going up to New Orleans with a cargo of wine from Bordeaux; but although she would, I doubt not, have been a legal capture, for breaking the blockade, the master was permitted to dispose of his cargo to our army, and an excellent thing he made of it, for the wine, which he must have purchased for about one shilling or one and sixpence a bottle, he charged us in general about four shillings for; we were glad, however, to get it at any price, and a most seasonable supply it was indeed. On one of our shooting excursions, an officer of ours fell in with a sow and two or three pigs, in the wood; he instantly fired at one of the pigs and killed it; but when going to pick it up, the sow set upon him with such fury, that he was glad to abandon his prize, and retreat with precipitation.

When the army landed near New Orleans, the 14th Light Dragoons had taken their saddles and other horse equipments with them, in hopes of being able to get mounted in the country; and which, being bulky, required a good large boat to bring off again. They were therefore put on board a considerable-sized one, with an officer of the regiment and a guard to protect them. On their way down towards the shipping, night overtook them before they could reach their destination, on which they pushed towards the shore, whether of an island or the mainland, I cannot say, in hopes of being more secure for the night; they consequently put on a sentry, and all lay down in the boat, to sleep. Soon afterwards, however, a boat came rowing rapidly alongside, and before the sentry could discover who or what they were, they boarded, and instantly made the party all prisoners.

The officer, I believe, when called on to deliver up his sword, was so annoyed at being trapped in such a manner, that he threw it into the lake, as far as he could fling it. The American officer who captured them was a lieutenant in their navy, and went by the name of Commodore Shiel (for every fellow is a commodore who commands even a few boats). He was so elated by his success on this occasion, and, I believe, by having taken another boat with stores, that he boasted to his prisoners, that he would take even Admiral Cochrane himself yet, before he left the country.

While we remained on Isle Dauphine, a commissary, with a sergeant and party of our men, were sent on shore, on the mainland, to shoot bullocks for the supply of the army. They had landed, and the commissary, with the sergeant and I think two men, went off into the neighbouring wood, leaving the two or three other men at the landing-place to protect the boat. Here again Mr Shiel made his appearance, quite suddenly and unexpectedly, having come round a jutting-point before the men were aware of his presence; he instantly, of course, made them prisoners, and, taking their arms from them, he put them on board their own boat, then, sending a part of his crew on board to manage it, despatched it for the American harbour. He now with a few more of his people went in search of the commissary and his party, whom he soon found; and they seeing resistance would be vain, when their own boat was departed, were compelled at once to surrender. He instantly put them into his own boat; and taking the commissary into the after-sheets alongside of himself, the sergeant and the other men were put forward to the head of the boat.

Whether any preconcerted scheme and signal had been agreed upon between the commissary and the sergeant, I do not know, but an opportunity soon after offering, the commissary gave the sergeant the wink, and instantly seizing Mr Shiel by the thighs, pitched him right overboard in an instant; the sergeant, at the same moment, seizing the stoutest of Shiel's men, and serving him in a like manner. The others being attacked by the remaining two men, at once surrendered, and, I believe, suffered themselves to be bound; and our people, having now resumed their arms and become masters of the boat, admitted Mr Shiel, who, I fancy, had clung to the boat to prevent his drowning, to come once more on board.

What became of the other man who was thrown over, I know not; whether he swam on shore, or was drowned, or was afterwards taken into the boat, I cannot tell; but the result was, that the great, the boasting Commodore Shiel, was brought to the island a prisoner, where he landed like a drowned rat, and quite chopfallen.

The commissary, who was a fine, stout, and gallant young fellow, spoke highly in praise of Tom Fukes, our sergeant, for his bravery and good management on the occasion.

At length the works being all completed for battering the fort, Colonel Smith was sent in with a flag of trace to demand its surrender. The commandant was quite undecided how to act, and asked the colonel what he, as a man of honour, would advise him to do.

"Why," says the colonel, "do you not see that our guns are now overlooking your whole work, and that we could, in a very short time, knock it down about your ears? I have no hesitation in telling you, that the rules of war will fully justify you in surrendering to such a superior force, and when the siege has advanced to such a point as it actually is." His arguments, together with the truth of his statements, at length overcame the courage and determination of Jonathan, and he instantly agreed to surrender, the garrison, afterwards becoming prisoners of war, marching out and laying down their arms on the glacis.

Thus, on the 12th February, this important fortification fell into our hands, together with 400 men of the 2nd Regiment of the United States, and either one or two American colours. This obstacle removed, every exertion was now made to advance up the lake to the attack of Mobile; but on the 14th, a vessel arrived with the unexpected, but cheering information, that peace had been concluded at Ghent between the two nations, and that it only required the ratification of Mr Maddison, the United States president. Of course, all farther operations of a warlike nature were suspended for the present, till it was known whether the treaty would be ratified or not. This ship also brought out the notification of our two generals, Lambert and Keane, being appointed Knights of the Bath. Some of our colonels also were included in the list, *viz*. Blakeny of the 7th, and Dickson of the Royal Artillery.

And now nothing was thought of but amusement, and making ourselves as comfortable as possible. But we began to get very short of provisions. Our people were therefore obliged to send to the Havannah, where they procured the strongest sort of beef I ever saw. It was not salted; but after the cattle had been killed, all the thin belly part had been cut round the whole bullock, in narrow stripes, of about two inches in width; this being laid, or hung up in the sun, which is extremely powerful in that country, it was dried without having the least offensive taste or smell, farther than a little rancidity, which was not by any means unpleasant; but when brought from on board, it had much more the appearance of coils of ropes (for it was coiled up in a similar manner) than provision for the use of man.

An *aide-de-camp* of General Lambert's, then Lieutenant, but now Major D Este, son of his Royal Highness the Duke of Sussex by Lady Augusta Murray, used frequently to join the shooting party of our acting quartermaster and myself; and, on one occasion, having obtained a canoe, a trip to the mainland was projected, for the purpose of shooting; accordingly we took two or three men with us, and started from the northernmost point of the island, that being the nearest to the main, which we saw before us, and not more than five or six miles distant.

It was considered the best mode of proceeding for us all to get into the boat, except one man, who was a famous wader, (having often accompanied us in our expeditions around the island,) and who was to wade as far out into the sea as he could, dragging the canoe after him. This he could do very easily, for she was quite light, and the water was exceeding shallow for a great distance into the sea. He continued towing us in this manner for about half a mile, when, being fairly up to his chin, he and we thought it was high time for him to come on board; but, in doing this, he gave her such a cant as turned her right over, and pitched us all into the water.

I luckily had my eye upon the man when he sprung to get into the canoe, and suspecting that she could not bear so rough a pull, was ready; and accordingly, when I saw her going, leaped out, without being plunged overhead, as all the others were. But all our rifles, &c. were pitched out, and of course sunk to the bottom, to which we were obliged to dive before we could get them up. This accident put a stop to our excursion, and we waded out again, looking extremely foolish. Nevertheless we ought to have been truly thankful to Providence that it occurred before we got out of our depth; for, with such a frail *bark*, it is more than probable some accident would have happened before our return, had not this prevented our farther progress.

Innumerable were our adventures of this nature, for the water was delightfully warm, and having no military occupation at the time, we could not find any better amusement. A party, indeed, suggested the getting up of theatricals, which being approved on all hands, workmen were instantly set about erecting the theatre-royal. Isle Danphine. This, of course, with the getting off of parts, occupied the managers and the other performers for some time; but at length all being ready, most excellent entertainments took place, following each other in quick succession. At some of these parties, American officers, who now often paid us visits, were highly entertained, and paid us high compliments, not only as to the splendour and magnificence of our theatrical representations, but to our ingenuity as displayed in hut-building, which, they said, even surpassed the architectural abilities of the Indians in that branch of the art,—a high compliment indeed!

Our Troops Embark For England

On the 5th March, the ratification of the treaty of peace, by Mr Maddison, arrived; and now all our thoughts were turned towards our dear native country. On the 15th also, all our poor fellows, who had been made prisoners by the Americans, joined us at this island, an exchange in consequence of peace having of course taken place. Many of these were strange-looking figures when they came among us, most of them having been stripped of great part of their uniforms, their caps particularly, and wearing *moccasins*, a sort of Indian sandals, instead of shoes or boots, and being so sunburnt as to be scarcely recognisable.

Major Mitchell told us that General Jackson had treated him exceeding harshly, because he did not choose to give the general such information respecting our numbers, &c as he wished. He also said he met with great insolence on his way up to Natchez, where the prisoners were kept, from the different parties of Kentucky men, and others, whom he met on their way down "to take a shoot," as they termed it, "at his countrymen." He met many thousands in this manner, so that 10,000 or 12,000 is the very lowest number that Jackson could have had for the defence of his lines.

I do not remember that we ever had Divine service performed during the period of this expedition except once or twice, and that about this time. Indeed the activity required of the army at all times, during the continuance of hostilities, almost necessarily precluded it. At this time I remember perfectly the preacher's text was, "*My son, give me thy heart.*" Alas! how few of the hearts of his hearers , were given at that time to Him who only had a right to demand them! I confess with shame and sorrow, that almost any trifle, however unworthy, possessed a greater interest in my heart than He who had formed it, and who alone is worthy of supreme regard.—The good Lord pardon this neglect, for Christ's sake!

The regiments now began to go on board the different ships, as fast as arrangements could be made to receive them; and when on board, they sailed at once without waiting for the others, there being now no danger of falling in with an enemy. The weather now began to grow exceedingly warm, which brought out alligators and snakes in abundance. The latter were extremely annoying, for they sometimes got into our very tents, and one on one occasion so frightened a captain of ours (who was not afraid of man) as to make him sprawl up the tent-pole to get out of its reach, roaring out at the same time most lustily for help. It was killed and put into a bottle of spirits, and I believe he brought it home. It was an exceeding small one, but with the most beautiful crimson, or rather pink-coloured wavy streak running down its back imaginable. We were told it was one of the most venomous of all the American reptiles, save probably the rattlesnake.

The thunder and lightning also became very frequent, and the former, I think, the most awfully grand I ever heard. It appeared to roll along just on the very tops of the pine-trees, many of which indeed were scathed to the very roots by the latter.

On the 31st March our turn came to go on board, and we were rejoiced to find that the *Dover*, our old friend, was to be our principal ship, the remainder of the men beyond what she could hold being sent on board the *Norfolk* transport. While we were preparing for sea, I took a boat and a party with a seine, and went on shore on a sandy point of the island, where I had not been before, and in a short time caught a fine load of fish, mostly grey mullet, with which we returned on board, greatly to the satisfaction of all those who shared in them.

Everything being now ready, we weighed and bid *adieu* to America on the 4th April, shaping our course for the Havannah, where our captain intended to call for various purposes, but principally to replenish his stock, which had begun to get exceedingly low.

On our passage thither we encountered a heavy gale, which detained us longer than we had calculated for our voyage. We did not reach that place till the 19th. Here we found ourselves once more in Espana, everything here being exactly like what you meet with in the mother country,—the same stink of oil, garlic, and dried fish.

Harry Smith of the 95th Rifles in America

STARTING FOR THE WAR IN AMERICA

My happiness of indolence and repose (after the conclusion of the Peninsular War) was doomed to be of short duration, for on the 25th of August (1814) I was in the Battle of Bladensburg, and at the capture of the American capital, Washington, Some thousands of miles distant. Colborne, my ever dear, considerate friend, then in command of his gallant Corps, the 52nd, sent for me, and said, "You have been so unlucky, after all your gallant and important service, in not getting your Majority, you must not be idle. There is a force, a considerable one, going to America. You must go. Tomorrow we will ride to Toulouse to headquarters; send a horse on tonight—it is only thirty-four miles—we will go there and breakfast, and ride back to dinner."

I said, very gratefully, "Thank you, sir; I will be ready. This is a kind act of yours;" but as I knew I must leave behind my young, fond and devoted wife, my heart was ready to burst, and all my visions for our mutual happiness were banished in search of the bubble reputation. I shall never forget her frenzied grief when, with a sort of despair, I imparted the inevitable separation that we were doomed to suffer, after all our escapes, fatigue, and privation; but a sense of duty surmounted all these domestic feelings, and daylight saw me and dear Colborne full gallop thirty-four miles to breakfast. We were back again at Castel Sarrasin by four in the afternoon, after a little canter of sixty-eight miles, not regarded as any act of prowess, but just a ride. In those days there were men.

On our arrival in Toulouse, we found my name rather high up—the third, I think—on the list of Majors of Brigade in the A.G.'s office desirous to serve in America. We asked kind old Darling who had put my name down. He said, "Colonel Elley," afterwards Sir John. He had known my family in early life, and was ever paternally kind to me. He had asked my ever dear friend, General Sir Edward Pakenham, to do so, which he readily did. Colborne then said, "My old friend Ross, who commanded the 20th Regiment while I was captain of the Light Company, is going. I will go and ask him to take you as his Major of Brigade."

Ross knew me on the retreat to Coruña, and the affair, in a military point of view, was satisfactorily settled. But oh! the heaviness of my heart when I had to impart the separation now decided on to my affectionate young wife of seventeen years old! She bore it, as she did everything, when the energies of her powerful mind were called forth, exclaiming, "It is for your advantage, and neither of us must repine. All your friends have been so kind in arranging the prospect before you so satisfactorily." At the word "friends" she burst into a flood of tears, which relieved her, exclaiming, "You have friends everywhere. I must be expatriated, separated from relations, go among strangers, while I lose the only thing on earth my life hangs on and clings to!"

Preparation was speedily made for our journey down the Garonne, which we performed in a small boat, accompanied by our kind friend Digby. My wife was to accompany me to Bordeaux, there to embark for England with my brother Tom, who had recently suffered excessively in the extraction of the ball he had received in his knee five years previously at the Coa. The great difficulty I had was to get my regimental pay (nine months being due to me), and I only did so through the kindness of our acting-paymaster, Captain Stewart, and every officer readily saying, "Oh, give us so much less the first issue, and let Smith have what would otherwise come to us." Such an act, I say, testifies to the mutual friendship and liberality we acquired amidst scenes of glory, hardship, and privation.

Before I left my old Brigade, the 52nd Regiment, the 95th Regiment (Rifle Brigade now), the 1st and 3rd Caçadores[1], with whom I had been so many eventful years associated—and I may say, most happily—all gave me a parting dinner, including the good fellows, the Portuguese, whom I never had any chance of seeing again. Our farewell dinner partook of every feeling of excitement. The private soldiers, too, were most affectionate, and I separated from all as from my home. The Portuguese are a brave, kind-hearted people, and most susceptible of kindness. We had also ten men a Company in our British Regiments, Spaniards, many of them the most daring of sharpshooters in our corps, who nobly regained the distinction attached to the name of the Spanish infantry in Charles V.'s time. I never saw better, more orderly, perfectly sober soldiers in my life, and as *vedettes* the old German Hussar did not exceed them. The 52nd Regiment I was as much attached to as my own corps, with every reason.

My old 1st Battalion embarked at Dover just before Talavera, 1,050 rank and file. During the war only 100 men joined us. We were now reduced to about 500. There was scarcely a man who had not been wounded. There was scarcely one whose knowledge of his duty as an outpost soldier was not brought to a state of perfection, and when they were told they must not drink, a drunken man was a rare occurrence indeed, as rare as a sober one when we dare give a little latitude. My old Brigade was equal to turn the tide of victory (as it did at Orthez) any day.

It was early in May when we left Castel Sarrasin, where we had been happy (oh, most happy!) for a month—an *age* in the erratic life we had been leading. We were quartered in the house of a Madame La Riviére, an excellent and motherly woman, a widow with a large family and only one son spared to her—the

---

1. The 3rd Caçadores at this period were commanded by a fine gallant soldier and a good fellow, but as he rejoiced in a name of unusual length—Senhor Manuel Terçeira Caetano Pinto de Silvuica y Souza—we gave him the much shorter appellation of "Jack Nasty Face," for he was an ugly dog, though a very good officer.—H.G.S.

rest had perished as soldiers. Never was there a more happy and cheerful family, and never did mother endeavour to soothe the acute feelings of a daughter more than did this good lady those of my poor wife. We often afterwards heard of her in Paris in 1815.

Our voyage down the Garonne in our little skiff was delightful. We anchored every night. In youth everything is novel and exciting, and our voyage was such a change after marching! The beauties of the scenery, and the drooping foliage on the banks of the river, added to our enjoyment. We landed each night at some town or village, and ever found a comfortable inn which could give us a dinner. After such privations as ours, the delight of being able to order dinner at an inn is not to be believed. On reaching Bordeaux, the most beautiful city I was ever in, I found I had only three or four days to prepare to reach the fleet and the troops embarked in the Gironde (a continuation of the Garonne), and that I was to embark on board His Majesty's ship the *Royal Oak*, 74, Rear-Admiral Malcolm, for the troops under General Ross were destined for a peculiar and separate service in America.

I did, of course, all I could to draw the attention of my poor wife from the approaching separation. There was a theatre, various spectacles, sights, etc., but all endeavour was vain to relieve the mind one instant from the awful thought of that one word "separation." Digby was most kind to her. He had an excellent private servant, who was to embark with her for London. My brother Tom was to her all a brother could be, and in the transport she was to proceed in were several old and dear Rifle friends going to England from wounds. I wished her to go to London for some time before going down to my father's, for the benefit of masters to learn English, etc.—for not a word could she speak but her own language, French, and Portuguese,—and to every wish she readily assented.

Time rolls rapidly on to the goal of grief, and afternoon arrived when I must ride twenty miles on my road for embarkation. Many a year has now gone by, still the recollection of that afternoon is as fresh in my memory as it was painful at the moment—oh, how painful! To see that being whose devotedness in the field of three years' eventful war, in a life of such hardship at the tender age of fourteen, had been the subject of wonder to the whole community, in a state bordering on despair, possessing, as she did, the strong and enthusiastic feelings of her country-women—who love with a force cooler latitudes cannot boast of—*this* was to me an awful trial, and although she had every prospect of care and kindness, to be *separated* conveyed to the sensitive mind of youth (For I was only twenty-four[2])— every anguish and horror that is to be imagined. I left her insensible and in a faint. God only knows the number of staggering and appalling dangers I had faced; but, thank the Almighty, I never was unmanned until now, and I leaped on my horse by that impulse which guides the soldier to do his duty.

I had a long ride before me on the noble mare destined to embark with me. On my way I reached a village where I received the attention of a kind old lady, who from her age had been exempt from having any troops quartered on her; but, the village being full of Rifle Brigade, Artillery, and Light Division fellows, the poor old lady was saddled with me. The Artillery readily took charge of my horse. The kind old grandmamma showed me into a neat little bedroom and left me.

I threw myself on the bed as one *alone* in all the wide world, a feeling never before experienced, when my eye caught some prints on the wall. What should they be but pictures in representation of the *Sorrows of Werther*, and, strange though it be, they had the contrary effect upon me to that which at the first glance I anticipated. They roused me from my sort of lethargy of grief and inspired a hope which never after abandoned me. The good lady had a nice little supper of *côtelettes de mouton*, and the most beautiful strawberries I ever saw, and she opened a bottle of excellent wine. To gratify her I swallowed by force all I could, for her kindness was maternal.

We soon parted forever, for I was on horseback before day-

2. He was nearly twenty-seven.

light, *en route* to Pauillac, a village on the Garonne, where we were to embark. On my ride, just at grey daylight, I saw something walking in the air. "It is like a man," I said, "certainly, only that men do not walk in the air." It advanced towards me with apparently rapid strides, and in the excited state of mind I was in, I really believed I was deluded, and ought not to believe *what I saw*. Suspense was intolerable, and I galloped up to it.

As I neared my aeronaut, I found it a man walking on stilts about twenty-five feet high. In the imperfect light and the distance, of course the stilts were invisible. The phenomenon was accounted for, and my momentary credulity in I did not know what called to mind stories I had heard recounted, evidently the results heated imaginations. This walking on stilts is very general in the deep sands of this country.

On reaching Pauillac, I found my trusty old groom West waiting for me. He led me to a comfortable billet, where my portmanteau, all my worldly property, and my second horse, which was to embark with me, were reported "All right, sir." Old West did not ask after "Mrs.," but he looked at me a thousand inquiries, to which I shook my head. I found a note for me at our military post-office from dear little Digby, as consolatory as I could expect.

I was detained two days at Pauillac, in the house of another widow, an elderly lady (all women in France of moderate or certain age were widows at this period). One morning I heard a most extraordinary shout of joyful exclamation, so much so I ran into the room adjoining the one I was sitting in. The poor old woman says, "Oh, come in and witness my happiness!" She was locked in the arms of a big, stout-looking, well-whiskered Frenchman. "Here is my son, oh! my long-lost son, who has been a [prisoner] in England from the beginning of the war."

The poor fellow was a *sous-officier* in a man-of-war, and, having been taken early in the war off Boulogne, for years he had been in those accursed monsters of inhuman invention, "the hulks," a prisoner. He made no complaint. He said England had no other place to keep their prisoners, that they were well fed when fed by the English, but when, by an arrangement with France at her own request, that Government fed them, they were half starved. The widow gave a great dinner-party at two o'clock, to which I was of course invited. The poor old lady said, "Now let us drink some of this wine: it was made the year my poor son was taken prisoner. I vowed it should never be opened until he was restored to me, and this day I have broached the cask."

The wine was excellent. If all the wine-growers had sons taken prisoners, and kept it thus until their release, the world would be well supplied with good wine in place of bad. Poor family! it was delightful to witness their happiness, while I could but meditate on the contrast between it and my wretchedness. But I lived in hope.

Sent Home With Dispatches

That afternoon, after seeing my horses off, I embarked in a boat, and I and all my personal property, my one portmanteau, reached the *Royal Oak*, at her anchorage a few miles below, about eight o'clock. I found General Ross had not arrived, but was hourly expected. We soldiers had heard such accounts of the etiquette required in a man-of-war, the rigidity with which it was exacted, etc., that I was half afraid of doing wrong in anything I said or did. When I reached the quarters, the officer of the watch asked my name, and then, in most gentlemanlike and unaffected manner, the lieutenant of the watch, Holmes (with whom I afterwards became very intimate), showed me aft into the Admiral's cabin.

Here I saw wine, water, spirits, etc., and at the end of the table sat the finest-looking specimen of an English sailor I ever saw. This was Admiral Malcolm, and near him sat Captain Dick, an exceedingly stout man, a regular representation of John Bull. They both rose immediately, and welcomed me on board in such an honest and hospitable manner, that I soon discovered the etiquette consisted in nothing but a marked endeavour to make us all happy. The fact is that army and navy had recently changed places. When I joined the army, it was just at a time when our navy, after a series of brilliant victories had destroyed at Trafalgar the navy of the world. Nine years had elapsed, and the glories of the army were so fully appreciated by our gallant brothers of the sea service, we were now by them regarded as the heroes whom I well recollect I thought them to be in 1805.

The Admiral says, "Come, sit down and have a glass of grog." I was so absorbed in the thought that this large floating ship was to bear me away from all so held so dear, that down I sat, and seized a bottle (gin, I believe), filled a tumbler half full, and then added some water. "Well done!" says the Admiral. "I have been at sea, man and boy, these forty years, but d—— me, if I ever saw a stiffer glass of grog than that in my life."

He afterwards showed me my cabin, telling me he was punctual in his hours. "I breakfast at eight, dine at three, have tea in the evening, and grog at night, as you see; and if you are thirsty or want anything, my steward's name is Stewart, a Scotchman like myself—tell the marine at the cabin door to call him and desire him to bring you everything you want." I shall never forget the kindness I received onboard the *Royal Oak*, and subsequently on board the *Menelaus* (commanded by poor Sir Peter Parker), and from every ship and every sailor with whom I became associated. Our navy are noble fellows, and their discipline and the respect on board for rank are a bright example to the more familiar habits of our army.

General Ross arrived next morning, with his A.D.C., Tom Falls, a captain in the 20th, and Lieut. De Lacy Evans (subsequently of great notoriety), both as good-hearted fellows as ever wore a sword. The fleet sailed in the afternoon. The troops all embarked in men-of-war, with the lower-deck guns out. We had on board a company of artillery; otherwise the force consisted of the 4th Regiment, the 44th, and the 85th. We had a very slow but beautiful passage to St. Michael's, one of the Western Islands, where, as Admiral Malcolm said, "that d——d fellow Clavering, the Duke of York's enemy, had the impudence to call on me," and we embarked live bullocks, fruit, and vegetables.

The parts capable of cultivation in this island are most fertile, and the inhabitants (all Portuguese) looked cheerful and happy. I could then speak Portuguese like a native. One day on shore I walked into a large draper's shop, where I was quite struck by the resemblance of the man behind counter to my old clerk, Sergeant Manuel. After some little conversation, I discovered he actually was his brother. At first I doubted it, but he fetched me a bundle of letters in which my name frequently appeared. It was an extraordinary rencontre, and my friend Señor Manuel's attention to me was very "*gostozo*" indeed.

We sailed for Bermuda in a few days. It was a long passage, but we had fine weather until we neared Bermuda, when we fell in with a violent thunderstorm, which carried away the mizen top-mast of the *Royal Oak*.

Much of my time was spent with my friend Holmes, and many is the time I have walked the quarter-deck with him. In any state of grief or excitement, someone who participates and sympathizes in your feeling is always sought for, and this warm-hearted fellow fully entered into all I must feel at the fate of my wife—a foreigner in a foreign land, to whom, though surrounded by many kind friends, everything was strange, everything brought home the absence of that being on whom her life depended.

On reaching Bermuda we found the 21st Regiment awaiting us, and a communication from the Admiral, Cochrane, commander-in-chief of the navy (who commanded on the coast of America 170 Pennons of all descriptions), that a battalion of marines was organised under Colonel Malcolm, the Admiral's brother, upwards of 800 strong, so that General Ross's force became respectable. The Admiral proposed to rendezvous in Chesapeake Bay so soon as possible.

Ross organized his force into three brigades, one commanded by Colonel Thornton, the second by Colonel Brooke, the third, which comprised all naval auxiliaries, by Colonel Malcolm. A brigade-major was appointed to each. I was put in orders deputy adjutant-general; Evans, deputy quartermaster-general. The price of things on this spot in the ocean was enormous; I, Evans, Macdougall, of the 85th, Holmes of the navy, etc., dined on shore at the inn one day, and were charged fifteen Spanish dollars for a miserable turkey; but the excellent fish called a "groper" made up for the price of the turkey.

General Ross left the troops here, and proceeded to join the naval commander-in-chief in a frigate. I was the only staff officer left with Admiral Malcolm, who was quite as much a soldier in heart as a sailor; he prided himself very much on having brought home the Duke of Wellington (when Sir A. Wellesley) from India, and he landed his army at Mondego Bay, before Vimiera. I never saw a man sleep so little: four hours a night was plenty, and half that time he would talk aloud in his sleep, and if you talked with him would answer correctly, although next morning he recollected nothing.

To get from the anchorage at Bermuda is difficult, and the wind was contrary, and appeared so likely to continue so, that the Admiral resolved on the boldest thing that was ever attempted, viz. to take the whole fleet through the North-east Passage—a thing never done but by one single frigate. There was only one man in the island who would undertake to pilot the 74 *Royal Oak* through. The passage is most intricate, and the pilot directs the helmsman by ocular demonstration, that is, by looking into the water at the rocks. It was the most extraordinary thing ever seen, the rocks visible under water all round the ship.

Our pilot, a gentleman, said there was only one part of the passage which gave him any apprehension. There was a turn in it, and he was afraid the *Royal Oak* was so long her bows would touch. When her rudder was clear, on my honour, there appeared not a foot to spare. The breeze was very light; at one period, for half an hour, it almost died away. The only expression the Admiral was heard to make use of was, "Well, if the breeze fails us, it will be a good turn I have done the Yankees." He certainly was a man of iron nerves. The fleet all got through without one ship touching. The Admiral's tender, a small sloop, ran on a rock, but was got off without injury.

At night, after the fleet was well clear (and the bold attempt was of every importance to the success of our expedition, which, as we now began to observe, evidently meditated the capture of Washington), we had rather a good passage to the mouth of the Chesapeake, where we met the Admiral Chief in Command and General Ross. We did not anchor, having a leading wind to take us up the bay. We were going ten knots when the frigate struck on the tail of a bank, with a crash like an earthquake; she got over, however, without injury. We anchored off the mouth of the Patuxen, the river which leads to Washington.

Next day all the Staff were assembled on board the *Tonnant* and all the Admirals came on board. We had present—Sir A. Cochrane, Admiral Cockburn (of great renown on the American coast), Admiral Malcolm, Admiral Codrington, captain of the fleet, and, if I recollect right, Sir T. Hardy, but he left us next day. After much discussion and poring over bad maps, it was resolved the force should sail up the serpentine and wooded Patuxen in the frigates and smaller vessels. This we did, and it was one of the most beautiful sights the eye could behold.

The course of the large river was very tortuous, the country covered with immense forest trees; thus, to look back, the appearance was that of a large fleet stalking through a wood. We went up as far as we could, and the Navy having very dexterously and gallantly burned and destroyed Commodore Barney's flotilla, which was drawn up to oppose our passage [19, 20 Aug.], the army was landed about thirty-six miles from Washington. I cannot say my dear friend General Ross inspired me with the opinion he was the officer Colborne regarded him as being. He was very cautious in responsibility—awfully so, and lacked that dashing enterprise so essential to carry a place by a *coup de main*. He died the death of a gallant soldier, as he was, and friendship for the man must honour the names of the brave.

We fell in with the enemy on our march, well posted on the eastern bank. We were told that the only approach to their position was by a bridge through the village of Bladensburg. The day we landed, a most awful spectacle of a man named Calder came in to give us information. He was given in my charge, the secret service department having been confided to me. The poor wretch was covered with leprosy, and I really believe was induced to turn traitor to his country in the hope of receiving medical [aid] from our surgeons, in the miserable state of disease he was in. If such was his object, he is partly to be pardoned. He was a very shrewd, intelligent fellow, and of the utmost use to us. He was afterwards joined by a young man of the name of Brown, as healthy a looking fellow as he was the reverse, who was very useful to us as a guide and as a scout.

When the head of the Light Brigade reached the rising ground, above the bridge, Colonel Thornton immediately proposed to attack, which astonished me [Battle of Bladensburg, 24 Aug.]. We old Light Division always took a good look before we struck, that we might find a vulnerable part. I was saying to General Ross we should make a feint at least on the enemy's left flank, which rested on the river higher up, and I was in the act of pointing out the position, guns, etc., when Colonel Thornton again proposed to move on. I positively laughed at him. He got furiously angry with me; when, to my horror and astonishment, General Ross consented to this isolated and premature attack.

"Heavens!" says I, "if Colborne was to see this!" and I could not refrain from saying, "General Ross, neither of the other Brigades can be up in time to support this mad attack, and if the enemy fight, Thornton's Brigade must be repulsed." It happened just as I said. Thornton advanced, under no cloud of sharpshooters, such as we Light Division should have had, to make the enemy unsteady and render their fire ill-directed. They were strongly posted behind redoubts and in houses, and reserved their fire until Thornton was within fifty yards. Thornton was knocked over, and Brown, commanding the 85th Light Infantry, and Captain Hamilton, a noble fellow from the 52nd, were killed, and the attack repulsed. "There," says I, "there is the art of war and all we have learned under the Duke given in full to the enemy!"

Thornton's Brigade was ordered to hold its own until the arrival of the brigade consisting of the 4th and 44th under Brooke, many men having dropped down dead on the march from the heat, being fat and in bad wind from having been so long on board.

As the brigades closed up, General Ross says, "Now, Smith, do you stop and bring into action the other two Brigades as fast as possible."

"Upon what points, sir?"

He galloped to the head of Thornton's people, and said, "Come on, my boys," and was the foremost man until the victory was complete. He had two horses shot under him, and was shot in the clothes in two or three places. I fed the fight for him with every possible vigour. Suffice it to say we licked the Yankees and took all their guns, with a loss of upwards of 300 men, whereas Colborne would have done the same thing with probably a loss of 40 or 50, and we entered Washington for the barbarous purpose of destroying the city. Admiral Cockburn would have burnt the whole, but Ross would only consent to the burning of the public buildings. I had no objection to burn arsenals, dockyards, frigates building, stores, barracks, etc., but well do I recollect that, fresh from the Duke's humane warfare in the South of France, we were horrified at the order to burn the elegant Houses of Parliament and the President's house.

In the latter, however, we found a supper all ready, which was sufficiently cooked without more fire, and which many of us speedily consumed, unaided by the fiery elements, and drank some very good wine also.[3] I shall never forget the destructive majesty of the flames as the torches were applied to beds, curtains, etc. Our sailors were artists at the work. Thus was fought the Battle of Bladensburg, which wrested from the Americans their capital Washington, and burnt its Capitol and other buildings with the ruthless firebrand of the Red Savages of

3. Ross wrote, "So unexpected was our entry and capture of Washington, and so confident was Madison of the defeat of our troops, that he had prepared a supper for the expected conquerors and when our advanced party entered the President's house, they found a table laid with forty covers" (*Dictionary of National Biography*, "Ross")

the woods. Neither our Admirals nor the Government at home were satisfied that we had not allowed the work of destruction to progress, as it was considered the total annihilation of Washington would have removed the seat of government to New York, and the Northern and Federal States were adverse to the war with England.

We remained two days, or rather nights, at Washington, and retired on the third night in a most injudicious manner. I had been out in the camp, and when I returned after dark, General Ross says, "I have ordered the army to march at night."

"Tonight?" I said. "I hope not, sir. The road you well know, for four miles to Bladensburg, is excellent, and wide enough to march with a front of subdivisions. After that we have to move through woods by a track, not a road. Let us move so as to reach Bladensburg by daylight. Our men will have a night's rest, and be refreshed after the battle. I have also to load all the wounded, and to issue flour, which I have also caused to be collected." (I had seized in Washington everything in the shape of transport, and Baxter, the Surgeon, brought away every wounded man who could travel.)

General Ross said, "I have made the arrangement with Evans, and we must march."

I muttered to myself, "Oh, for dear John Colborne!"

We started at nine, and marched rapidly and in good order to Bladensburg, where we halted for about an hour to load the wounded. The barrels of flour were arranged in the streets, the heads knocked in, and every soldier told to take some. Soldiers are greedy fellows, and many filled their haversacks. During a tedious night's march through woods as dark as chaos, they found the flour far from agreeable to carry and threw it away by degrees. If it had not been for the flour thus marking the track, the whole column would have lost its road. Such a scene of intolerable and unnecessary confusion I never witnessed.

At daylight we were still not three miles from Bladensburg. Our soldiers were dead done, and so fatigued, there was nothing for it but to halt and bring into play the flour, which was soon set about, while we Staff were looking out like a Lieutenant of the Navy in chase, to see the Yankees come down upon us with showers of sharpshooters. Thanks to their kind consideration they abstained from doing so, but we were very much in their power.

I now began to see how it was that our Light Division gentlemen received so much credit in the army of the dear Duke. I recommend every officer in command to avoid a night march as he would the devil, unless on a good road, and even thus every precaution must be taken by all staff officers to keep up the communications, or regularity cannot be ensured. I have seen many night marches, but I never yet saw time gained, or anything beyond the evil of fatiguing your men and defeating your own object. You may move before daylight, *i.e.* an hour or two, if the nights are light. By this means, about the time the column requires collection, daylight enables you to do it. You have got a start of your enemy, your men are in full vigour either to march rapidly or, in case of difficulty, to fight. But avoid night marches. However, owing to their want of knowledge of the art of war, the enemy on this occasion allowed us to get to our boats perfectly unmolested.

On one of the days we were near Washington a storm came on, a regular hurricane. It did not last more than twenty minutes, but it was accompanied by a deluge of rain and such a gale that it blew down all our piles of arms and blew the drums out of camp. I never witnessed such a scene as I saw for a few minutes. It resembled the storm in Belshazzar's feast,[4] and we learnt that even in the river, sheltered by the woods, several of our ships at anchor had been cast on their beam ends.

We gave out we were going to Annapolis, and thence to Baltimore to re-act the conflagration of Washington, and the bait took. Some American gentlemen came in under a flag of truce, evidently to have a look at us, but avowedly to ask how private

---

4. The biblical account of Belshazzar's feast (Daniel v.) does not mention a storm. Sir H. Smith's mental picture was no doubt derived from engravings of Martin's representation of the scene.

property had been respected. Their observations were frustrated by our vigilance. I was sent out to receive them, and nothing could exceed their gentlemanlike deportment. I loaded them with questions about roads, resources, force, etc., etc., at Annapolis and Baltimore. It was evident they took the bait, for that night we heard their army was off in full force to Annapolis, leaving us quietly to get down to our ships. We made arrangements for the care and provisioning of the wounded we had left at Bladensburg, and the attention and care they received from the Americans became the character of a civilized nation.

We reached our landing place unmolested, and at our leisure embarked our army, which began to suffer very much from dysentery. A long sea voyage is the worst possible preparation for long and fatiguing marches. The men are fat, in no exercise, have lost the habit of wearing their accoutrements, packs, etc.—in short, they are not the same army they were on embarkation. Before our men left the Gironde, thirty miles a day would have been nothing to them.

General Ross, just before we went on board, sent for me (there never was a more kind or gallant soldier), and said, "Smith, the sooner I get my dispatch home the better. As you know, it is nearly ready, and as poor Falls, my A. D. C., is too unwell, it is my intention you should be the bearer of my dispatches, and that Falls should go home for the benefit of his health." This most unexpected arrangement set me on the *qui vive* indeed, I had not been in England for seven years. Wife home, country, all rushed in my mind at once. The general said, "A frigate is already ordered by the Admiral."

This day my information man, Calder the Leper, came to me, and told me that Brown had been taken and would be hung. I was much distressed. Although one cannot admire a traitor to his country, yet I was some degree of gratitude in his debt, and I said, "Well, Calder, but can we do nothing to save him?"

"Well, now I calculate that's not to be denied, and if I hear General Ross say, 'If I catch that rascal Brown, I will hang him like carrion,' he may be saved, for I would go at once among our people (they will not injure me), and I will swear I heard General Ross say so."

I immediately went to the general. On the first view of the thing, his noble nature revolted at making an assertion he never intended to abide by. At length, however, to save the poor wretch's life, he consented, and in course of a desultory conversation with Calder, dovetailed the words required into it. I saw Calder catch at it. When he left the general's tent, he said to me, "Well, now, I calculate Brown may yet live many years."

He left us that night with a purse of money and a long string of medical instructions for the benefit of his health from one of our surgeons. "Ah," says he, "this will save *me*" (meaning the medical advice); "I can save Brown."

I had an hieroglyphical note from him brought by a slave, just before I sailed [30? Aug. 1814], to say "All's right, you may reckon." I told this story afterwards to the Prince Regent. He was exceedingly amused.

The *Iphegenia* frigate, Captain King, was to take me home, and Captain Wainwright of the *Tonnant* was to be the bearer of the naval dispatches. Sir Alexander Cochrane, Admiral Cockburn, and Evans, burning with ambition, had urged General Ross to move on Baltimore. The general was against it, and kindly asked my opinion. I opposed it, not by opinions or argument, but by a simple statement of facts.

"1. We have, by a ruse, induced the enemy to concentrate all his means at Baltimore.

"2. A *coup de main* like the conflagration of Washington may be effected once during a war, but can rarely be repeated.

"3. The approach to Baltimore Harbour will be effectually obstructed."

"Oh," says the general, "so the Admirals say; but they say that in one hour they would open the passage."

I laughed. "It is easier said than done, you will see, General." (The passage defied their exertions when tested.)

"4. Your whole army is a handful of men, and the half of them are sick from dysentery.

"5 Your success in the attack on Washington is extraordinary, and will have a general effect. Your success on Baltimore would add little to that effect, admitting you were successful, which I again repeat I doubt, while a reverse before Baltimore would restore the Americans' confidence in their own power, and wipe away the stain of their previous discomfiture."

General Ross says, "I agree with you. Such is my decided opinion."

"Then, sir, may I tell Lord Bathurst you will not go to Baltimore?"

He said, "Yes." I was delighted, for I had a presentiment of disaster, founded on what I have stated.

The day we were to sail in the *Iphegenia* as I left the *Tonnant* kind-hearted General Ross, whom I loved as a brother, accompanied me to the gangway. His most sensible and amiable wife was at Bath. I promised to go there the moment I had delivered my dispatches, and of course I was charged with a variety of messages. In the warmth of a generous heart he shook my hand, and said, "A pleasant voyage, dear Smith, and thank you heartily for all your exertions and the assistance you have afforded me. I can ill spare you."

My answer was, "Dear friend, I will soon be back to you, and may I assure Lord Bathurst you will not attempt Baltimore?"

"*You may.*" These were the last words I ever heard that gallant soul utter. He was over-ruled: attempted Baltimore [12 Sept. 1814], failed, and lost his noble life. A more gallant and amiable man never existed, and one who, in the continuance of command, would have become a general of great ability. But few men, who from a regiment to a brigade are suddenly pushed into supreme authority and have a variety of conflicting considerations to cope with—navy, army, country, resources, etc., are at the outset perfectly at home.

The *Iphigenia* had a most extraordinary passage from the

Chesapeake to our anchorage at Spithead. We were only twenty-one days. The kindness I received from Captain King I shall never forget The rapidity of our voyage was consonant to my feelings and in perfect accordance with my character.

He Receives Orders to Return To America

Wainwright and I started from the George Inn, Portsmouth, which I well knew, with four horses at five o'clock. I do not know what he considered himself; but I was of opinion that, as the bearer of dispatches to Government, I was one of the greatest men in England. Just before we started, our outfit merchant and general agent, tailor, etc., by name Meyers, who had been very civil to me going out to South America, begged to speak to me. He said, "I find the *Iphegenia* is from America, from the Chesapeake: that little box under your arm contains, I see, dispatches."

"Well," I said, "what of that?"

"If you will tell me their general purport, whether *good news* or *bad*, I will make it worth your while, and you may secure some pounds for a refit."

At first I felt inclined to knock him down. On a moment's reflexion I thought, "every one to his trade," so I compromised my feelings of indignation in rather a high tone of voice, and with "I'd see you d—d first; but of what use would such general information be to you?"

He, a knowing fellow, began to think *the pounds* were in my thoughts, so he readily said, "I could get a man on horseback in London two hours before you, and good news or bad on 'Change' is my object. Now do you understand?"

I said, "Perfectly, and when I return to America I shall expect a capital outfit from you for all the valuable information I have afforded you. Goodbye, Meyers."

Oh! the delight of that journey. I made the boys drive a furiously good pace. D—— me, if I had rather be beating off a lee-shore in a gale, tide against me! The very hedgerows, the houses, the farms, the cattle, the healthy population all neatly clothed, all in occupation; no naked slaves, no burned villages, no starving, wretched inhabitants, no trace of damnable and accursed war! For seven years, an immense period in early life, I had viewed nothing beyond the seat of a war, a *glorious* war, I admit, but in that glory, death in its most various shapes, misery of nations, hardships, privations, wounds, and sickness, and their concomitants. The wild excitement bears a soldier happily through.

My career had been a most fortunate one. Still the contrast around me was as striking as the first appearance of a white and clothed man to a naked savage. The happy feeling of being in my native land once more, in health and in possession of every limb, excited a maddening sensation of doubt, anxiety, hope, and dread, all summed up in this—"Does your young wife live? Is she well?" Oh the pain, the hope, the fear, and the faith in Almighty God, who had so wonderfully protected me, must have turned the brain if endurance had continued, for I had never heard of her since we parted.

At twelve o'clock we were in London, and drove to Downing Street, where I lodged my dispatches; then we sought out a bivouac, I and poor Falls. The navy man was off to the Admiralty. Every inn was full near Downing Street, at least where I desired to be. At last we got to the Salopian Coffee-house in Parliament Street. The waiter said, "One spare bedroom, sir; nothing more."

"Oh, plenty!" we said. We had been feasting on the road on that indigenous-to-England luxury of bread, butter, cream, and tea. All we wanted was an hour or two's sleep, for, at that time of night, as to finding any one, we might as well have been back in America!

The chambermaid said, "Only one room, sir."

"Plenty," we said.

"But only one bed, gentlemen!"

"Plenty," we said. "Bring up the portmanteau, West." When we got to the room and proceeded (West and I) to divide this copious bed into two by hauling half the clothes on the floor, according to our custom of seven years, the astonishment of the poor chambermaid is not to be described. We bundled her out and were asleep before a minute.

By daylight I was in a hackney coach, and drove to the British (the Scotch) barracks of my old Rifle comrades. There I asked the porter the name of any officer he knew. At last he stammered out some. "Colonel Ross?"

"What regiment?" says I.

"He had a green jacket when he came up."

I knew it was my dear friend John Ross.

"Where is the room?" I said.

"Oh, don't disturb the gentleman, sir; he is only just gone to bed."

Says I, "My friend, I have often turned him out, and he shall quickly be broad awake now."

He showed the room. In I bolted.

"Halloa, Ross, stand to your arms."

"Who the devil are you?"

"Harry Smith," I said; "fall in."

Our joy was mutual.

"Well, but quiet, John; is my wife alive and well?"

"All right, thank God, Harry, in every respect as you would wish. I was with her yesterday."

"Where, John? where?"

"In Panton Square; No. 11."

It is difficult to decide whether excess of joy or of grief is the most difficult to bear; but seven years' fields of blood had not seared my heart or blunted my naturally very acute feelings, and I burst into a flood of tears. "Oh, thank Almighty God."

Soon I was in Panton Square, with my hand on the window of the coach, looking for the number, when I heard a shriek, "*Oh Dios, la mano de mi Enrique!*"

Never shall I forget that shriek; never shall I forget the effusion of our gratitude to God, as we held each other in an embrace of love few can ever have known, cemented by every peculiarity of our union and the eventful scenes of our lives. Oh! you who enter into holy wedlock for the sake of connexions-

tame, cool, amiable, good, I admit—you cannot feel what we did. That moment of our lives was worth the whole of your apathetic ones for years. We were unbounded in love for each other, and in gratitude to God for all His mercies. Poor little Pug was, in her way, as delighted to see me as her more happy mistress, and many an anecdote was told me of her assisting by moaning pitifully when my wife grieved aloud, as she was sometimes induced to do.

This happy reunion effected, I was off to Downing Street, where my Lord Bathurst received me in the kindest manner, and said, "The intelligence you bring is of such importance, the Prince Regent desires to see you. We will go immediately."

I said, "My Lord, be so good as to allow me to take the map I brought you."

"It is here." And off we started to Carlton House. We were shown into a large room where Lord Bathurst fortunately left me for half an hour, which enabled me somewhat to allay my excited imagination and return to the battlefields. I was soon deep in thought, when a sort of modesty came over me at the idea of approaching England's (*actual*) king. I gave my head a toss, saying, "I never quailed before the dear Duke of Wellington, with his piercing eye, nor will I now, and General Ross begged of me to talk;" for His Royal Highness, the story went, complained that "the bearer of dispatches will never talk." Johnny Kincaid says I was an impudent fellow." At any rate, I determined, if I saw His Royal Highness really desired me to be communicative, I would not be unready.

While I was forming all sorts of plans for both attack and defence, in came Lord Bathurst: "The Prince will see you."

So I said, "My Lord, if we were in camp, I could take your Lordship all about, but I know nothing of the etiquette of a court."

So he says, "Oh, just behave as you would to any gentleman; His Highness's manner will soon put you at ease. Call him 'Sir,' and do not turn your back on him."

"No," says I, "my Lord, I know that; and my profession is one of 'show a good front.'"

In we went to the Prince's dressing-room, full of every sort of article of dress, perfumes, snuff-boxes, wigs, every variety of article, I do believe, that London could produce.

His Highness rose in the most gracious manner, and welcomed me to his presence by saying, "General Ross strongly recommended you to my notice[5] as an officer who can afford me every information of the service you come to report, the importance of which is marked by the firing of the Parliament and Tower guns you now hear."

I could not refrain from smiling within myself at Harry Smith of the Light Division sitting with the Prince Regent, and all London in an uproar at the news he brought. I was perfectly thunderstruck at the military questions the Prince asked me. He opened a map of America, and then referred to the plan of Washington I had brought home, with the public buildings burnt marked in red. He asked the name of each, and in his heart I fancied I saw he thought it a barbarian act. On all other topics he spoke out. I said it was to be regretted a sufficient force had not been sent to hold Washington.

His Highness said, "What do you call a sufficient force?"

I said, "14,000 men." He very shrewdly asked on what I based such an opinion. I talked of navy, of population, etc., and perfectly satisfied His Highness I did not give an opinion at random.

He asked a variety of questions, and laughed exceedingly when I told him the anecdote of Calder's promising to save Brown. When I got up to leave the room, and was backing out, His Highness rather followed me, and asked if I were any relation of his friend, Sir —— Smith, in Shropshire.

---

5. From Major-General Ross to Earl Bathurst

Tonnant in the Patuxent, Aug. 30, 1814.

"Captain Smith, assistant adjutant-general to the troops, who will have the honour to deliver this dispatch, I beg leave to recommend to your lordship's protection, as an officer of much merit and great promise, and capable of affording any further information that may be requisite" (Given in W. James's *Military Occurrences of the Late War* (1818), 2.)

I said, "No."

He then said, "I and the Country are obliged to you all. Ross's recommendations will not be forgotten, and, Bathurst, don't forget this officer's promotion." It was the most gentlemanlike and affable interview I could possibly imagine.

That evening I was to dine at Lord Bathurst's at Putney. I never met a more amiable-mannered man than Lord Bathurst; and his secretary, Punch Greville[6], volunteered to drive me out in his tilbury. When I got into the drawing-room, who should be there but my dear friend Lord Fitzroy Somerset? He had been recently married. At dinner I sat between Lady Fitzroy and an elderly gentleman whose name I did not know, and, as the party was small, and I the lion, every one induced me to talk. Lord Fitzroy and I across the table got back into Spain; and, of course, as I regarded the Duke of Wellington as something elevated beyond any human being, and I was in high spirits, I did not hesitate to launch forth our opinion of him. The elderly gentleman who sat next me said, "I am very glad to hear you speak in such raptures of the Duke. He is my brother."

I laughed, and said, "I have not exceeded in anything, to the best of my judgement."

After dinner Lord Fitzroy Somerset and I had a long talk. He had travelled after Toulouse, in a little carriage from Bordeaux to Cadiz with the Duke, and their conversation frequently turned on the army. Fresh are the words on my mind at this moment. "The Duke often said to me, 'The Light, 3rd and 4th Divisions were the *élite* of my army, but the Light had this peculiar perfection. No matter what was the arduous service they were employed on, when I rode up next day, I still found a *division*. They never lost one half the men other divisions did.'"

I was delighted, for this was what we so prided ourselves on. I have often heard our soldiers bullying one another about the number such a Company had lost, always attaching discredit

---

6. Charles Cavendish Fulke Greville (1794-1865), Clerk to the Privy Council from 1821; author of the *Greville Memoirs*; known to his friends as Punch, or the Gruncher (*Dict. Nat. Biog.*).

to the loss. It was a peculiar feeling, and one which actuated them throughout the war, combined with the most undaunted bravery and stratagem as sharpshooters. But I must revert to domestic matters.

My wife had refused all the entreaties of my family to leave London before my return. She availed herself of masters, and saw so many friends daily. She had a forcible impression that I should not be long away. We started for Bath, and I wrote to my father to come to London in a few days, and we would return with him to Whittlesea. We found poor Mrs. Ross in the highest spirits at the achievement of our arms under her husband. Poor thing! at that very moment of her excessive happiness he was in a soldier's bloody grave.

The delight of our journey to and from Bath is not to be described. Everything was modern, novel, and amusing to my wife: every trifle called forth a comparison with Spain, although she admitted that there was no comparison between our inns and the Spanish *posadas*, so accurately described in *Gil Blas*. No brutal railroads in those days, where all are flying prisoners. We dined where we liked; we did as we liked. At the last stage back into London, my wife, in looking at a newspaper (for she began to read English far better than she spoke), saw my promotion to the rank of major—"The reward," she said, "of our separation."

On arrival in London we found my father had arrived from the country. I had not seen him for seven years. In this period *he* had been deprived of his devoted wife, leaving him eleven children, *I*, of a mother; for everything that word comprises in its most comprehensive sense I had lost. Our pleasure at meeting, as may be supposed, was excessive, while we mingled our tears for the departed. As my wife had just come off a journey, and it was late in the afternoon, I would not show her to my father until she was dressed for dinner: a little bit of vanity and deception on my part, for I led him to believe she was of the stiff Spanish school, as stately as a swan and about as proud as a peacock. She liked the fun of the deception, and promised to dress in full Spanish costume, and act up to the supposition.

In she came, looking—oh! if I could but describe her! but in place of acting either the swan or the peacock, she bounded into my father's arms, who cried like a child, between joy, admiration, astonishment and delight at seeing so young and beautiful a creature who had gone through so much, and showed a heart evidently framed for love.

She was now nearly eighteen, but a woman—not a girl, and certainly a person of most distinguished appearance, especially in her Spanish costume; not handsome, if beauty depends on regularity of features, for she had the dark complexion of the fairer part of her countrywomen, but with a colour beneath the clearest skin of olive which gave a lustre to her countenance—a countenance illumined by a pair of dark eyes possessing all the fire of a vivid imagination, and an expression which required not the use of speech. Her figure was beautiful, and never was any costume so calculated to exhibit it in perfection and in all its graces as that of her native land.

She had a profusion of the darkest brown hair; teeth, though not regular, as white as pearls; with a voice most silvery and sweet in conversation, and she would sing the melancholy airs and songs of constancy of her country (so celebrated for them) with a power and depth of voice and feeling peculiar to Spain. Her foot and ankle were truly Spanish. She danced beautifully. Thus it was that the natural grace of her figure and carriage was developed, while the incomparable elegance and simplicity of her manner was a thing not to be forgotten, rarely to be met with. Her pronunciation of English at this period was most fascinating, and when she wanted a word, the brilliancy and expression of the eye would supply it. It flashed perpetually as she spoke, and filled up the intervals her slight knowledge of our language could not supply.

She was animated and intelligent, with a touching tone of confidence and gentleness which made the hearer a willing listener to her words, but still her meaning was supplied by her vivid countenance. Such was the being my affectionate and kind-hearted father held locked in his paternal embrace, the faithful wife of his son. They were ever afterwards friends in every sense of the word, and, as he was the best and boldest horseman I ever saw in my life, and she could ride beautifully and any horse they were inseparable.

Poor "Old Chap," my war horse, which, together with her Andalusian "Tiny," I had sent to him, was dead, but, the morning after our arrival at Whittlesea, we were taken to the stall. There was Tiny in such condition The meeting between my wife and the horse was, as she said, that of compatriots in a foreign land. It was rendered still more amusing by the little pug and horse equally recognizing each other, for many a day had Tiny carried Pug. (My dear little thoroughbred horse I had so cried over was still alive and fresh, but alas! I had grown out of his memory. He was standing in the next stall, and had acquired the name of "Old Jack.")

My wife let Tiny loose, to the alarm of my father, who expected to see him fly off full speed into his garden, which he prided himself on considerably. To his astonishment, and to mine too (for my father told me the groom could barely lead him), she says, "Now don't make a noise, and he will follow me like a dog," which he did into the drawing-room, Occasionally licking her hand or face when she allowed him. The saddle, however, was soon on him, and, as if proud to show off that he was broken in like a Mameluke's, she figured him so that few Mamelukes, *jerreed*[7] in hand, could have touched her with effect.

In the midst of [happiness] I had the most melancholy visit to pay to my mother's tomb. If ever souls on earth could commune, I was so fascinated by the hallowed spot, which contained all which I so adored from my infancy, my consoler, my counsellor, my guide to the holy hill of God, I really believed I heard her speak when I prayed over her head and again vowed my promises at parting. Oh! that she could have lived to know my elevation, my being the bearer of dispatches to our King,

---

7. Byron, *The Giaour*.
Swift as the hurled on high jerreed,
Springs to the touch his startled steed.

that she could have seen my wife, that she could have shared, Heaven bless her, in the happiness of her children around! This one blank was for the moment all I lacked. I consoled myself that while we were revelling on earth with every uncertainty before us, she, my mother, was in heaven, where I dare firmly believe she is, for God is gracious and bountiful.

On my return from that hallowed and sacred spot, I found letters from the Horse Guards. The first was to order me to London immediately, the next was to tell me what I little anticipated. General Ross, contrary to his own opinion and his promise, had attempted Baltimore [12 Sept.], failed, as I anticipated, and lost his gallant life from not following the dictates of his own good sense and ability. My dear friend Sir Edward Pakenham was appointed to succeed him. I was appointed A.A.G. to the increased force going out!

I had been nearly three weeks under the paternal and hospitable roof—my only holiday for years—when that blighting word "separation" was again to be imparted to my faithful and adoring wife; and, cut off from all social ties of happiness and endearment, I was again immediately, in the very middle of winter, to encounter the stormy Atlantic and all the horrors of war in the distance. It is only a repetition of the former tale to talk of my poor wife's distress. It was agreed she was to accompany me to London, and my father was to bring her back; and twenty-four hours later, while brothers and sisters re-echoed each others' promises, and indeed feelings, of affection, we started back to London, with hearts as heavy as they were light coming down.

I little thought then of what I had to go through, witness, and endure, but, if I had, my task would still have been to affect a cheerfulness in the prospect of more promotion which, I avow candidly, I did not feel. However, I was a soldier, and as much wedded to my profession and a sense of duty as any man, so I lit up my torch of hope and did all in my power to cheer and comfort her I so loved.

On our arrival in London I immediately went to poor dear Sir Edward Pakenham, who was delighted to see me, and said that we must be in Portsmouth in a few days, and that the *Statira* frigate was waiting for us. I then sought out Macdougall of the 85th, who before I left the Army had been acting, in place of sick Falls, as A.D.C. to poor Ross, and I readily learned all that occurred before the service lost that gallant soldier.

My firm and faithful friend John Robb, surgeon of the 95th when I joined, was appointed Inspector-General of Hospitals, and he and I agreed to send our baggage by coach, and go down together to Portsmouth in a post chaise on Sunday afternoon, for the *Statira* was to sail on Monday. Old West was started off per coach, and at three o'clock on Sunday, the—November, the horrible scene of parting was again to be endured. It was less painful to me than the first, I admit, for my dear wife was now known and beloved by all my family; but to her the dread of separation, and separation for the exploits of war, was as painful as before, and, when I tore myself from her, which I was literally obliged to do, that heart must be hard indeed that was not, as mine was, ready to break.

I can see her now, with her head resting on the chimney-piece (as I left the room, and took a farewell glance) in a state bordering on despair. My father, too, was awfully overcome. In a few minutes I was rolling on my road to Portsmouth, deeply absorbed, I admit, but my companion Robb was a man of strong mind, of whom I had a high opinion, and not to appear desponding before him, I exerted all my energy and began to talk of my plans on my return. Robb said the only thing I ever heard him say that I thought would have been as well unsaid—"Oh, that's capital! a fellow going out to be killed by an American Rifleman, talking of what he will do when he comes back!" Now, such is the perversity of human nature, this so put up my blood, that grief and anguish were mitigated in a determined spirit of opposition.

We arrived at the George at twelve at night, and found West, who reported all right. We found an order directing us to be on board by ten o'clock, as the ship would get under weigh at twelve, and we knew that our men of war are punctual fellows.

129

The next morning, at breakfast, we directed old West to parade our portmanteaus. My kit had increased just double, *viz*. I had now two portmanteaus.

"Here they are, sir," says West.

"Why, that is not mine, West!" He overhauled it, and soon agreed with me. We went to the coach; there was no other. So I opened it, and, to my horror, in place of my things, it contained the dirty linen of a Frenchman and his silk stockings and evening pantaloons, etc, etc. Upon a little inquiry from poor old West, we learned that two coaches were loading at the same time, one for Dover, the other for Portsmouth. It was evident, therefore, my red coats were in company with my French friend. In my portmanteau were all my boots, my uniform, and my flannel waistcoats. We were to embark immediately, and I had nothing for it but to go to my *friend*, and tell him, "Now's the time for the outfit I have lost my portmanteau." He very kindly undertook to write to Charing Cross and send back the Frenchman's, and in three weeks after the failure at New Orleans my portmanteau was sent out to me by my dear friend John Bell.

It is a very odd coincidence that, on my first going abroad to South America, I lost my kit and all my large stock of silver given me by my poor mother—some teaspoons, etc. On that occasion I never recovered anything.

THE EXPEDITION AGAINST NEW ORLEANS

We soon reached our frigate, and oh, so crowded as she was!—Sir Edward Pakenham and all his staff, the commanders of the Engineers and Artillerymen with their staff, and about thirty passengers! The most of us slept in cots in the steerage. Young D'Este,[8] the real Duke of Sussex, was a fund of great amusement, the most gentlemanlike, kind-hearted young fellow possible, affable to a degree, and most unpretending; but he had a thirst for obtaining information, I never beheld before. Con-

8. Augustus Frederick (b. 1794), only son of Augustus Frederick; Duke of Sussex (son of George III.), by his marriage with Lady Augusta Murray. The two children of this marriage, when disinherited by the Royal Marriage Act, took the name D'Este.

sequently he laid himself open to some very peculiar replies to his queries. He proved himself on shore, like all the royal family, a gallant and intrepid soldier, and the best shot with a rifle for a youth that I have almost ever seen. He attached himself passionately to me on board and on shore, and if he ever became Elector of Hanover, I was to have been his secretary.

We had a very agreeable party of gallant old Peninsular soldiers, and dear Sir Edward was one of the most amusing persons imaginable—high-minded and chivalrous fellow in every idea, and, to our astonishment, very devoutly inclined; and Major Gibbs, who was afterwards killed on the same day as Sir Edward, was a noble fellow.

The *Statira* was a noble frigate; she had a full complement of men, and was in crack order, having every individual on board but the individual who had put her in—that Irish Captain Stackpoole, of duelling celebrity, who had very shortly before been shot in the West Indies by a Lieutenant of another ship on whom he saddled a quarrel originating in an occurrence when both were middies. The Lieutenant denied all recollection of it to no purpose. Stackpoole insisted on his going out. The Lieutenant, it was said, had never fired a pistol in his life, but at the first shot Stackpoole fell dead.

I never saw a body of officers and men more attached than these were to their last captain. Everyone had some anecdote of his kindness and ability as a seaman. The propensity which cost him his life can be attributed, I am firmly of opinion, to nothing but a strain of insanity upon that particular subject alone. His prowess as a shot with a pistol, it was asserted, was inconceivable, but "the battle is not always to the strong."

On this voyage I had two opportunities of writing to my wife, or, rather, sending her the sheets of a sort of journal which she made me promise to keep. Our Captain, Swaine, a neighbour of mine in Cambridgeshire, was of the old school, and made everything snug at night by shortening sail, to the great amusement of poor Stackpoole's crew, accustomed to carry on night and day. But for this, we should have been off the mouth of the Mississippi at the time when Sir Edward was informed a fleet and his army would rendezvous for an assault on New Orleans. As it was, we did [not] reach the fleet until [25 Dec.] three days after the landing had been effected, and our army under Major-General Sir J. Keane, now Lord Keane (as noble a soldier as our country ever produced) had sustained a sharp night-attack. Stovin, the A.G., had been shot through the neck, and I was at the head of the department.

I never served under a man whose good opinion I was so desirous of having as Sir Edward Pakenham, and proud was I to find I daily succeeded. I was always with him, and usually lay in my cloak in his room. The second day after we reached General Keane [28 Dec.], the army was moved up to reconnoitre the enemy's position, or to attack, if we saw it practicable. I was that day delighted with Sir Edward: he evinced an animation, a knowledge of ground, of his own resources and the strength of the enemy's Position, which reminded us of his brother-in-law, *our Duke*. The staff were very near the enemy's line, when I saw some rifle-men evidently creeping down and not farther off than a hundred yards, and so I very abruptly said, "Ride away, Sir Edward, behind this bank, or you will be shot in a second. By your action you will be recognized as the commander-in-chief, and some riflemen are now going to fire."

The American riflemen are very slow, though the most excellent shots. My manner was so impressive he came away. As we were returning that evening he called me to him, and said, "You gentlemen of the Craufurd school" (he was very fond of our old Light Division) "are very abrupt and peremptory in your manner to your generals. Would you have spoken to Craufurd as you did to me today?"

I said, "Most certainly, for if I had not, and one of us had been killed or wounded, and he became aware I observed what I did when I spoke to you, he would have blown me up as I deserved. He taught us to do so. How my dear friend Sir Edward laughed!

We soon found that, with our Present force, the enemy's position was impregnable. A brigade was, however, daily expected, under Sir J Lambert. While we were looking out with our telescopes, Sir Edward turned very abruptly to me, and said, "Now for a Light Division [opinion]. What do you say, Smith, as to the Practicability of an attack on the enemy's line?"

I replied, "His position is strong—his left being on an impracticable morass, his right on the Mississippi; the ground is a dead flat, intersected with ditches which will impede our troops. The enemy has, literally, a breastwork, and plenty of men upon it, and their fire will sweep the plain with unerring precision, causing us great loss; for we can produce no fire, flank or otherwise, to render them uneasy or unsteady. As yet, the enemy has not occupied the opposite bank of the river. He has two armed vessels in the river. We must destroy these as soon as possible, possess the right bank of the Mississippi, enfilade the enemy's position with our fire (the width of the river being only from seven to eight hundred yards), and, so soon as we open a fire from the right bank, we should storm the work in two, three, or more columns."

"You Rifle gentlemen have learnt something, I do believe."

I did not know at the time whether he said this in jest or not, for he was a most light-hearted fellow; but, when we got back to the house we put up in, he sent for me. He had a plan of the works and position of the enemy before him, and said, "Smith, I entirely [concur] in all you said in the field today. In the meanwhile, we must facilitate our communications by roads in our rear, etc. I will erect batteries and destroy the ships, and, when the batteries are complete, they shall open on the enemy. If they can destroy the enemy's defence in any part, or silence the fire of his batteries, the army shall storm at once. Lambert's arrival is very uncertain."

I remarked, if Lambert's arrival was so uncertain, we had no alternative, and under any circumstances the ships must be destroyed and batteries erected, whether Lambert's force arrived or not.

We succeeded in destroying one ship—we *might have* destroyed both. We erected several batteries, their defences principally sugar-casks,—for here on the plain, on the banks of the Mississippi, if you dug eight inches, water followed: hence to erect batteries with earth was impracticable, and we had not sufficient sand-bags. The defences of our batteries, therefore, were reported complete on the night of the 31st December. The army was formed into two columns of attack—one threatening the right flank, the other the left, and a party was hid in the reeds in the morass on the enemy's left flank with orders to penetrate, if possible, and disturb the enemy's left.

At daybreak on the 1st of January, 1815, our troops were formed, and our batteries opened. They had not the slightest effect on the enemy. On the contrary, his shot went through the imperfect defence, caused our noble artillerymen great loss, and silenced our batteries. Hence there was no attack, and Sir Edward still more strenuously adhered to the necessity of occupying the right bank of the river. The troops were withdrawn, except such strong picquets as were left to protect the guns in the [batteries].

Poor Sir Edward was much mortified at being obliged to retire the army from a second demonstration and disposition to attack, but there was nothing for it. It came on to rain in the evening, and was both wet and cold. Sir Edward slept in a little house in advance of his usual quarters. He told me to stay with him, and all his staff to return to the usual house. He said, "Smith, those guns must be brought back; go and do it."

I said, "It will require a great many men."

"Well," he says, "take 600 from Gibbs's Brigade."

Off I started. The soldiers were sulky, and neither the 21st nor the 44th were distinguished for discipline—certainly not of the sort I had been accustomed to. After every exertion I could induce them to make, I saw I had no chance of success—to my mortification, for to return and say to Sir Edward I could not effect it, was as bad as the loss of a leg. However, the night was wearing, and my alternative decided; so I told him as quietly as I could. He saw I was mortified, and said nothing, but jumped up in his cloak, and says, "Be so good as to order my horse, and go on and turn out Gibbs's whole brigade quietly."

They were under arms by the time he arrived, and by dint of exertion and his saying, "I am Sir Edward Pakenham, etc., and commander-in-chief," as well as using every expression to induce officers and soldiers to exertion, just as daylight appeared he had completed the task, and the Brigade returned to its ground.

As we were riding back Sir Edward said, "You see, Smith, exertion and determination will effect anything."

I was cruelly mortified, and said, "Your excitement, your name, your energy, as commander-in-chief with a whole brigade, most certainly has done that which I failed in with 600 men, but I assure you, Sir Edward, I did all I could."

His noble heart at once observed my misery. He said, 'I admire your mortification; it shows your zeal. Why I barely effected, with all the exertion of the commander-in-chief, and, as you say, a brigade, what I expected you to do with one-fourth of the men!" He might have added, "and I did with some of the guns what you dare not even recommend to me." Oh, how I was comforted! To fall in his estimation would have been worse than death by far.

In a day or two we had information that Lambert's Brigade, the 7th Fusiliers and the 43rd Foot, [had arrived]. Two such corps would turn the tide of a general action. We were rejoiced! Sir Edward then made preparations to cross the river, and so to widen a little stream as to get the boats into the Mississippi. The story has been too often told to repeat. Lambert's Brigade landed, and, upon a representation made to Sir Edward by Major Sir G. Tylden, who was an assistant adjutant-general like myself, but a senior officer (as kind a fellow as ever lived), that, in Stovin's incapacity from his wound, he must be at the head of the Adjutant-General's Department, Sir Edward sent for me. "Smith," he said, "it was my intention you should have remained with me, Tylden with Lambert; but he claims his right as senior officer. You would not wish me to do an unjust thing when the claim is preferred?" I said, with my heart in my mouth, "Certainly not, sir." (I do believe I was more attached to Sir Edward, as a soldier, than I was to John Colborne, *if possible*.)

"You must, therefore, go to Lambert. I will [enter] this arrangement in Orders; but, rely on it, I shall find enough for you and him to do too."

The night of the 7th January, the rivulet (or *bayou*, as then called) was reported dammed, and the boats above the dam ready for the banks of the Mississippi to be cut. The water within the banks was higher than the level of the water in the bayou, consequently so much water must be let into the bayou as to provide for the level. In the meanwhile, the enemy had not been asleep. They had been apprised of our operations to establish ourselves on the right bank; they had landed the guns from the second ship (which we ought to have destroyed), and were respectably in possession of that which we must turn them out of. Sir Edward Pakenham went to inspect the *bayou*, the boats, etc. I heard him say to the engineer, "Are you satisfied the dam will bear the weight of water which will be upon it when the banks of the river are cut?"

He said, "Perfectly."

"I should be far more so if a second dam was constructed."

The engineer was positive.

After dark the banks were cut, the dam went as Sir Edward seemed to anticipate, and the delay in repairing it prevented the boats being got into the river in time for the troops under Colonel Thornton of the 85th to reach their ground and make a simultaneous attack with the main body, according to the plan arranged. Sir John Lambert's Brigade, the *élite* 7th Fusiliers and 43rd, were in reserve. Sir Edward said, "Those fellows would storm anything, but, indeed, so will the others, and when we are in New Orleans, I can depend upon Lambert's Reserve."

We were all formed in three columns [8 Jan.], about 6000 British soldiers and some sailors: a column under Colonel Renny of the 21st were destined to proceed on the banks of the river and right of the enemy, and carry a powerful battery which enfiladed the whole position: General Keane's Brigade was to assail the enemy's right-central position: General Gibbs's Brigade to attack well upon the enemy's left: General Lambert's Brigade to be in reserve nearer Gibbs's Brigade than Keane's.

About half an hour before daylight, while I was with General Lambert's column, standing ready, Sir Edward Pakenham sent for me. I was soon with him. He was greatly agitated. "Smith, most commanders-in-chief have many difficulties to contend with, but surely none like mine. The dam, as you heard me say it would, gave way, and Thornton's people will be of no use whatever to the general attack."

I said, "So impressed have you ever been, so obvious is it in every military point of view, we should possess the right bank of the river, and thus enfilade and divert the attention of the enemy; there is still time before daylight to retire the columns now. We are under the enemy's fire so soon as discovered."

He says, "This may be, but I have twice deferred the attack. We are strong in numbers now comparatively. It will cost more men, and the assault must be made."

I again urged delay. While we were talking, the streaks of daylight began to appear, although the morning was dull, close, and heavy, the clouds almost touching the ground. He said, "Smith, order the rocket to be fired."

I again ventured to plead the cause of delay. He said, and very justly, "It is now too late: the columns would be visible to the enemy before they could move out of fire, and would lose more men than it is to be hoped they will in the attack. Fire the rocket, I say, and go to Lambert."

This was done. I had reached Lambert just as the stillness of death and anticipation (for I really believe the enemy was aware of our proximity to their position) [was broken by the firing of the rocket]. The rocket was hardly in the air before a rush of our troops was met by the most murderous and destructive fire of all arms ever poured upon column. Sir Edward Pakenham galloped past me with all his staff, saying, "That's a terrific fire, Lambert."

I knew nothing of my general then, except that he was a

most gentlemanlike, amiable fellow, and I had seen him lead his brigade at Toulouse in the order of a review of his Household Troops[9] in Hyde Park. I said, "In twenty-five minutes, general, you will command the army. Sir Edward Pakenham will be wounded and incapable, or killed. The troops do not get on a step. He will be at the head of the first brigade he comes to, and what I say will occur."

A few seconds verified my words. Tylden came wildly up to tell the melancholy truth, saying, "Sir Edward Pakenham is killed. You command the army, and your brigade must move on immediately."

I said, "If Sir Edward Pakenham is killed, Sir John Lambert commands, and will judge of what is to be done." I saw the attack had irretrievably failed. The troops were beat back, and going at a tolerable pace too; so much so, I thought the enemy had made a sortie in pursuit, as so overpowering a superiority of numbers would have induced the French to do. "May I order your brigade, sir, to form line to cover a most irregular retreat, to apply no other term to it, until you see what has actually occurred to the attacking columns?"

He assented, and sent me and other staff officers in different directions to ascertain our condition. It was (summed up in few words) that every attack had failed; the commander-in-chief and General Gibbs and Colonel Renny killed; General Keane, most severely wounded; and the columns literally destroyed. The column for the right bank were seen to be still in their boats, and not the slightest impression had been made on the enemy.

Never since Buenos Ayres had I witnessed a reverse, and the sight to our eyes, which had looked on victory so often, was appalling indeed. Lambert desired me, and every staff officer he could get hold of; to go and reform the troops, no very easy matter in some cases. However, far to the rear, they (or, rather, what were left) were formed up, Sir John meanwhile wondering whether, under all the circumstances, he ought to attack. He

---

9. Sir J. Lambert was always in the Guards, and prided himself on being Adjutant of the Grenadier Guards, as his eldest son now is.—H.G.S. (1844)

very judiciously saw that was impossible, and he withdrew the troops from under a most murderous fire of round shot.

Soon after this we heard the attack on the right bank, which succeeded easily enough. The extent of our loss was ascertained: one-third.

The Admirals came to the outlying picquet-house with faces as long as a flying jib: a sort of Council of War was held. I had been among the troops to find out how the pluck of our soldiers [stood]. Those who had received such an awful beating and been so destroyed were far from desirous to storm again. The 7th and 43rd, whose loss had been trifling, were ready for anything, but their veteran and experienced eyes told them affairs were desperate. One Admiral, Coddrington, whose duty as captain of the field was to have seen it supplied with provisions, said, "The troops must attack or the whole will be starved."

I rather saucily said, "Kill plenty more, Admiral; fewer rations will be required." A variety of opinions were agitated. I could observe what was passing in Sir J. Lambert's mind by the two or three remarks he made.

So up I jumped, and said, "General, the army are in no state to renew the attack. If success now attended so desperate an attempt, we should have no troops to occupy New Orleans ; our success even would defeat our object, and, to take an extreme view, which every soldier is bound to do, our whole army might be the sacrifice of so injudicious an assault."

A thick fog was coming on. I said, "We know the enemy are three times our number. They will endeavour immediately to cut off our troops on the right bank, and we may expect an attack in our front. The fog favours us, and Thornton's people ought to be brought back and brought into our line. The army is secure, and no farther disaster is to be apprehended."

The general was fully of my opinion, as was every officer of experience. I think my noble friend, "fighting MacDougall," was the only one for a new fight. That able officer, Sir A. Dickson, was sent to retire Thornton, and, thanks to the fog, he succeeded in doing so unmolested, though, at the very time our people were crossing the river, a powerful body of the enemy (as I had supposed they would) were crossing to dislodge Thornton; and the woods on the right bank so favoured their species of warfare, that Thornton would have met the fate he did at Bladensburg but for Lambert's cool judgement. This was my view of the position then, and it is now.

The number of wounded was three times what the Inspector-General Robb was told to calculate on, but never did officer meet the difficulties of his position with greater energy, or display greater resources within himself. He was ably assisted in the arrangements of boats, etc., by that able sailor, Admiral Malcolm, and I firmly assert not a wounded soldier was neglected.

Late in the afternoon I was sent to the enemy with a flag of truce, and a letter to General Jackson, with a request to be allowed to bury the dead and bring in the wounded lying between our respective positions. The Americans were not accustomed to the civility of war, like our old *associates* the French, and I was a long time before I could induce them to receive me. They fired on me with cannon and musketry, which excited my choler somewhat, for a round shot tore away the ground under my right foot, which it would have been a bore indeed to have lost under such circumstances. However, they did receive me at last, and the reply from General Jackson was a very courteous one.

After the delivery of the reply to General Lambert, I was again sent out with a fatigue party a pretty large one too—with entrenching tools to bury the dead, and some surgeons to examine and bring off the wounded. I was received by a rough fellow—a Colonel Butler, Jackson's adjutant general. He had a drawn sword, and no scabbard. I soon saw the man I had to deal with. I outrode the surgeon, and I apologized for keeping him waiting; so he said, "Why now, I calculate as your doctors are tired; they have plenty to do today." There was an awful spectacle of dead, dying, and wounded around us.

"Do?" says I, "why this is nothing to us Wellington fellows! The next brush we have with you, you shall see how a brigade of the Peninsular army (arrived yesterday) will serve you fellows out with the bayonet. They will lie piled on one another like round shot, if they will only stand."

"Well, I calculate you must get at 'em first."

"But," says I, "what do you carry a drawn sword for?"

"Because I reckon a scabbard of no use so long as one of you Britishers is on our soil. We don't wish to shoot you, but we must, if you molest our property; we have thrown away the scabbard."

By this time our surgeon had arrived. There were some awful wounds from cannon shot, and I dug an immense hole, and threw nearly two hundred bodies into it. To the credit of the Americans not an article of clothing had been taken from our dead except the shoes. Everybody was straightened, and the great toes tied together with a piece of string. A more appalling spectacle cannot well be conceived than this common grave, the bodies hurled in as fast as we could bring them. The Colonel, Butler, was very sulky if I tried to get near the works. This scene was not more than about eighty yards away from them, and, had our fellows rushed on, they would not have lost one half; and victory would have been ours.

I may safely say there was not a vital part of man in which I did not observe a mortal wound, in many bodies there were three or four such; some were without heads; there were others, poor fellows, whom I recognized. In this part of America there were many Spaniards and Frenchmen. Several soldiers and officers gathered round me, and I addressed them in their own language. Colonel Butler became furious, but I would not desist for the moment, and said, "The next time we meet, Colonel, I hope to receive you to bury your dead."

"Well, I calculate you have been on that duty today," he said. God only knows I had, with a heavy heart. It was apparently light enough before him, but the effort was a violent one.

At night it was General Lambert's intention to withdraw his line more out of cannon shot, for we were on a perfect plain, not a mound as cover, and I and D'Este (His Royal Highness, as

I used to call him) were sent to bring back Blakeney's Brigade. Blakeney was as anxious a soldier in the dark as he was noble and gallant when he saw his enemy. He would fain induce me to believe I did not know my road. I got all right, though, with the aid of D'Este, who, if the war had lasted, would have made as able a soldier as his ancestor George the Second. I did not regard myself; though, as Marlborough, who was little employed on any retiring duty.

That night I lay down in my cloak, in General Lambert's room, at twelve o'clock, so done that all care or thought was banished in sleep Before daylight [9 Jan.] I awoke to the horror of the loss of the man I so loved, admired, and esteemed, and to feelings of a soldier under such melancholy circumstances. Those feelings could be but momentary. It was my duty to jump on my horse and see what was going on at our post, which I did, after returning Almighty God thanks. Thence to the hospital to render the Inspector whatever aid he required in orderlies, etc. Robb deserved and received the highest encomiums for the arrangements, which secured every care to our wounded.

In returning from the outposts, I met General Lambert. Upon my assuring him everything was perfectly quiet, he said, "I will now ride to the hospital."

"I was just going there, sir, and will ride with you."

The general said, "You must have been pretty well done last night, for I did not see you when I lay down."

"Yes, I had a long day, but we Light Division fellows are used to it."

"Smith, that most amiable man and cool and collected soldier, Secretary Wylly, will take home the dispatches of the melancholy disaster, and of the loss of his General and patron, and I offer for your acceptance my Military Secretaryship."

I laughed, and said, "Me, sir! I write the most illegible and detestable scrawl in the world."

"You can, therefore," he mildly said, "the more readily decipher mine. Poor Pakenham was much attached to you, and strongly recommended you to me."

I had borne up well on my loss before, but I now burst into a flood of tears, with—"God rest his gallant soul." From that moment to the present, dear General Lambert has ever treated me as one of his own family. Our lamented general's remains were put in a cask of spirits and taken home by his military secretary, Wylly, who sailed in a few days with dispatches of no ordinary character—a record of lamentable disaster, and anything but honour to our military fame.

It was resolved to re-embark the army, and abandon the idea of further operations against the city of New Orleans, for the enemy had greatly added to his strength in men and works on both banks of the river. This decision was come to although we were expecting reinforcements, the 40th and 27th Regiments, and that noble soldier, Sir Manley Power. The enemy continually cannonaded our position, and caused us some loss. We were obliged, however, to maintain an advance position to cover effectually the embarkation of all the impedimenta, etc., invariably giving out as a ruse that we were only disencumbering ourselves of wounded, sick, etc.

I was sent in, also, with a flag of truce to propose an exchange of prisoners. Two companies of the 21st Regiment and many of our Riflemen had crowned the works, and, not being supported by the rush of the column, of course were taken prisoners. (It was all very well to victimise[10] old Mullins[11]; the fascines, ladders, etc., could have been supplied by one word which I will not name[12], or how could these two companies have mounted the works?) Similarly we had several men of theirs taken the night the enemy attacked General Keane[13].

---

10. *i.e.* make a scapegoat of.

11. Colonel Mullins was blamed for not having the ladders and fascines ready.

12. Pluck?

13. After that attack I have always been of opinion that General Keane should have occupied the narrow neck of land behind the deep ditch which ran across from the river to the morass, and was afterwards (but then not at all) so strongly fortified by the enemy. I admit there were many, very many objections, but I still maintain there were more important reasons for its occupation, since our Army had been shoved into such a position, for, to begin from the beginning, it ought never to have gone there.—H.G.S.

In the negotiations for this exchange I was always met by a Mr. Lushington, General Jackson's military secretary, a perfect gentleman, and a very able man. He was well known in London, having been Under Secretary of the Legation. I never had to deal with a more liberal and clear-headed man. His education had not been military, however, and in conversation, by questions, etc., I always induced him to believe we had no intention of abandoning our attempts.

On the afternoon when our prisoners were mutually delivered, I said, "We shall soon meet in New Orleans, and after that in London." He was evidently impressed with the idea that we meant to attack again, and I led him to the supposition that a night attack would succeed best. We parted excellent friends, and shook hands, and many notes of courtesy passed between us afterwards.

So soon as it was dark [18 Jan.] our troops began to move off and about twelve o'clock all were well off the ground, and the picquets were retired. As we were so engaged, the enemy heard us, and in a moment opened a fire along their line, evidently under the belief that our night attack was actually about to be made. We retired, up to our necks in mud, through a swamp to our boats, and the troops and stores, etc. were all embarked in three days without interruption, or any attempt whatever, on the part of the enemy.

Thus ended the second awful disaster in America it had been my lot to be associated with—Buenos Ayres and New Orleans. In the circumstances of both, many military errors may be traced. But in the case of Buenos Ayres, Whitelock is more abused than he merits. General Leveson-Gower was the great culprit; an overbearing, disobedient man, whose first disobedience, like Adam's, entailed the misfortune. He was ordered, when advancing on Buenos Ayres, not to engage the enemy before it was invested. He did engage, beat them, and might, in the *mêlée* have possessed the city.

That he neglected, and he ought to have been dismissed our service, probably with greater justice than Whitelock, whose orders were wantonly disobeyed, and the church of San Domingo shamefully surrendered. Had it been held, as it might, it would have enabled Whitelock, from the base of his other success, to have made an attempt either to rescue the force in San Domingo, or again to have moved against the city. Whitelock's plan of attack was injudicious, too many columns, no weight and ensemble, and when he knew the city was fortified at every street, he should have effected regular lodgements and pushed forward from their base. The troops behaved most gallantly.

Poor dear Sir Edward Pakenham, a hero, a soldier, a man of ability in every sense of the word, had to contend with every imaginable difficulty, starting with the most unwise and difficult position in which he found the army. By perseverance, determination, and that gallant bearing which so insures confidence, he overcame all but one, which he never anticipated, a check to the advance of British soldiers when they ought to have rushed forward. There was no want of example on the part of officers.

The fire, I admit, was the most murderous I ever beheld before or since; still two companies were successful in the assault, and had our heaviest column rushed forward in place of halting to fire under a fire fifty times superior, our national honour would not have been tarnished, but have gained fresh lustre, and one of the ablest generals England ever produced saved to his country and his friends.

In General Lambert's dispatches he was good enough to mention me.[14]

END OF THE AMERICAN WAR

After the army was somewhat refreshed, an attempt on Mobile was resolved on, for which purpose the fleet went down

---

14. From Major-General Lambert to Earl Bathurst.
His Majesty's Ship *Tonnant* off Chandeleur's Island,
January 28, 1815.
Major Smith, of the 95th Regiment now acting as Military Secretary, is so well known for his zeal and talents, that I can with great truth say that I think he possesses every qualification to render him hereafter one of the brightest ornaments of his profession.

to the mouth of Mobile Bay. Here there was a wooden fort of some strength, Fort Bowyer, which some time previously had sunk one of two small craft of our men-of-war which were attempting to silence it. It was necessary that this fort should be reduced in order to open the passage of the bay. It was erected on a narrow neck of land easily invested, and required only a part of the army to besiege it. It was regularly approached, and when our breaching batteries were prepared to burn or blow it to the devil, I was sent to summon it to surrender.

The Americans have no particular respect for flags of truce, and all my Rifle education was required to protect myself from being rifled and to procure a reception of my flag. After some little time I was received, and, upon my particular request, admitted into the fort, to the presence of Major Lawrence, who commanded, with five companies, I think, of the 2nd Regiment. I kept a sharp look-out on the defences, etc., which would not have resisted our fire an hour. The major was as civil as a vulgar fellow can be. I gave him my version of his position and cheered him on the ability he had displayed.

He said, "Well, now, I calculate you are not far out in your reckoning. What do you advise me to do? You, I suppose, are one of Wellington's men, and understand the rules in these cases."

"This," I said, "belongs to the rule that the weakest goes to the wall, and if you do not surrender at discretion in one hour, we, being the stronger, will blow up the fort and burn your wooden walls about your ears. All I can say is, you have done your duty to your country, and no soldier can do more, or resist the overpowering force of circumstances."

"Well, if you were in my situation, you would surrender, would you?"

"Yes, to be sure."

"Well, go and tell your General I will surrender tomorrow at this hour, provided I am allowed to march out with my arms and ground them outside the fort."

"No," I said, "I will take no such message back. My General, in humanity, offers you terms such as he can alone accept, and the blood of your soldiers be on your own head."

He said, "Well, now, don't be hasty."

I could see the major had some hidden object in view. I said, therefore, "Now, I tell you what message I will carry to my General. You open the gates, and one of our companies will take possession of it immediately, and a body of troops shall move up close to its support; then you may remain inside the fort until tomorrow at this hour and ground your arms on the glacis."

I took out pen and ink, wrote down my proposition, and said; "There, now, sign directly and I go."

He was very obstinate, and I rose to go, when he said, "Well, now, you are hard upon me in distress."

"The devil I am," I said. "We might have blown you into the water, as you did our craft, without a summons. Goodbye."

"Well, then, give me the pen. If I must, so be it;" and he signed.

His terms were accepted, and the 4th Light Company took possession of the gate, with orders to rush in in case of alarm. A supporting column of four hundred men were bivouacked close at hand with the same orders, while every precaution was taken, so that, if any descent were made from Mobile, we should be prepared, for, by the major's manner and look under his eyebrows, I could see there was no little cunning in his composition. We afterwards learned that a force was embarked at Mobile, and was to have made a descent *that very night*, but the wind prevented them. We were, however, perfectly prepared, and Fort Bowyer was ours.

The next day [12 Feb.] the major marched out and grounded his arms. He was himself received very kindly on board the *Tonnant*, and his officers were disposed of in the fleet. The fellows looked very like French soldiers, for their uniforms were the same, and much of the same cut as to buttons, belts, and pipeclay.

In a few days after the capture of this fort the *Brazen* sloop-of-war arrived with dispatches [14 Feb.] The preliminaries of peace were signed, and only awaited the ratification of the President, and until this was or was not effected, hostilities were to cease. We were all happy enough, for we Peninsular soldiers saw that neither fame nor any military distinction could be acquired in this species of *milito-nautico*-guerrilla-plundering-warfare.

I got a letter from my dear wife, who was in health and composure, with my family all in love with her, and praying of course for my safe return, which she anticipated would not be delayed, as peace was certain. I for my part was very ready to return, and I thanked Almighty God from my heart that such fair prospects were again before me, after such another series of wonderful escapes.

Pending the ratification, it was resolved to disembark the whole army on a large island at the entrance of Mobile Bay, called Isle Dauphine[15]. This was done. At first we had great difficulty in getting anything like fresh provisions; but, as the sea abounded with fish, each regiment rigged out a net, and obtained a plentiful supply. Then our biscuit ran short. We had abundance of flour, but this began to act on the men and produce dysentery. The want of ovens alone prevented our making bread.

This subject engrossed my attention for a whole day, but on awakening one morning a sort of vision dictated to me, "There are plenty of oyster-shells, and there is sand. Burn the former and make mortar, and construct ovens." So I sent on board to Admiral Malcolm to send me a lot of hoops of barrels by way of a framework for my arch. There was plenty of wood, the shells were burning, the mortar soon made, my arch constructed, and by three o'clock there was a slow fire in a very good oven on the ground. The baker was summoned, and the paste was made, ready to bake at daylight. The Admiral, dear Malcolm, and our generals were invited to breakfast, but I did not tell even Sir John

---

15. Cope's order of events is as follows: Disembarkation of troops on Ile Dauphine, Feb. 8; surrender of Fort Bowyer, Feb. 11 ; arrival of news of the preliminaries of peace, Feb. 14. According to the text, the disembarkation on Ile Dauphine would appear to have followed the peace-news. There is no inconsistency, however. Only one Brigade (the 4th, 21st, and 44th Regiments) was employed in reducing Fort Bowyer. This Brigade disembarked on Ile Dauphine after the capture of the fort, the rest of the army having disembarked previously.

Lambert why I had asked a breakfast-party. He only laughed and said, "I wish I could give them a good one!"

Oh, the anxiety with which I and my baker watched the progress of our exertions! We heard the men-of-war's bells strike eight o'clock. My breakfast-party was assembled. I had an unusual quantity of salt beef and biscuit on the table, the party was ready to fall to, when in I marched at the head of a column of loaves and rolls, all piping hot and as light as bread should be. The astonishment of the Admiral was beyond all belief, and he uttered a volley of monosyllables at the idea of a soldier inventing anything. Oh, how we laughed and ate new bread, which we hadn't seen for some time! At first the Admiral thought I must have induced his steward to bake me the bread as a joke, when I turned to Sir John and said, "Now, sir, by this time tomorrow every Company shall have three ovens, and every man his pound and a half of bread."

I had sent for the quartermasters of corps; some started difficulties, but I soon removed them. One said, "Where are we to get all the hoops?"

This was, I admit, a puzzle. I proposed to make the arch for the mortar of wood, when a very quick fellow, Hogan, quartermaster of the Fusiliers, said, "I have it: make a bank of sand, plaster over it; make your oven; when complete, scratch the sand out." In a camp everything gets wind, and Harry Smith's ovens were soon in operation all over the island. There were plenty of workmen, and the morrow produced the bread.

The officers erected a theatre, and we had great fun in various demi-savage ways. Bell, the quartermaster-general, dear noble fellow, arrived, and a Major Cooper, and, of some importance to me, my stray portmanteau. I was half asleep one morning, rather later than usual, having been writing the greater part of the night, when I heard old West say, "Sir, sir."

"What's the matter?"

"Thank the Lord, you're alive."

"What do you mean, you old ass?"

"Why, a navigator has been going round and round your

tent all night; here's a regular road about the tent." He meant an alligator, of which there were a great many on the island. The young ones our soldiers used to eat. I tasted a bit once; the meat was white, and the flavour like coarsely-fed pork.

In this very tent I was writing some very important documents for my general; the sandflies had now begun to be very troublesome, and that day they were positively painful. I ever hated tobacco, but a thought struck me, a good volume of smoke would keep the little devils off me. I called my orderly, a soldier of the 43rd, and told old West, who chawed a pound a day at least, to give him plenty of tobacco, and he was to make what smoke he could, for of two evils this was by far the least. The old Peninsular soldiers off parade were all perfectly at home with their officers, and he puffed away for a long time while I was writing, he being under my table. After a time he put his head out with a knowing look, and said, "If you please, sir, this is drier work than in front of Salamanca, where water was not to be had, and what's more, no rum neither."

I desired West to bring him both rum and water.

"Now, your honour, if you can write as long as I can smoke, you'll write the history of the world, and I will kill all the midges."

The ratification at length arrived [5 March], and the army was prepared to embark. Sir John Lambert, Baynes his *aide-de-camp*, and I were to go home in the Br*a*zen sloop-of-war, with a Captain Stirling, now Sir James, who was ultimately the founder of the Swan River Settlement. A more perfect gentleman or active sailor never existed: we have been faithful friends ever since. As many wounded as the *Brazen* could carry were embarked, and we weighed with one of our noble men-of-war.

As soon as the word was given, we sailed to Havannah for fresh provisions. We spent a merry week there, when Stirling and I were inseparable. We were all feted at the house of a Mr. Drake, nominally a wealthy merchant, but actually in every respect a prince. I never saw a man live so superbly. He put carriages at our disposal; one for Sir John Lambert, and one for me and

Stirling. He was married to a Spanish woman, a very ladylike person, who played and sang beautifully. I could speak Spanish perfectly, and the compatriot connexion I told her and her maiden sisters of made us friends at once.

My spare time, however, was spent in the house of the Governor, Assuduco, who had a daughter so like my wife in age, figure, etc., and speaking English about as much as she could, I was never so much amused as in her society; and my wife and she corresponded afterwards. We stayed in the Havannah a week, and the public drives brought us all back again to the Prado of Madrid. Although the beauty of the ladies of the capital was wanting, the costumes were equally elegant.

The celebrated Woodville, the cigar manufacturer, asked us to a public breakfast at his house, four or five miles out of the city. He was about six feet two, as powerful a man as I ever saw; his hair in profusion, but as white as snow ; the picture of health, with a voice like thunder. He was rough, but hospitable, and after breakfast showed us the various processes of his manufactory, and the number of hands each went through.

"Now," says he, "Sir John, I have another sight to show you, which few men can boast of." With his fingers in his mouth, he gave a whistle as loud as a bugle, when out ran from every direction a lot of children, of a variety of shades of colour, all looking happy and healthy. Not one appeared above twelve or thirteen. "Ah," he said, "report says, and I believe it, they are every one of them my children."

"Count them," he said to me.

I did; there were forty-one. I thought Stirling and I would have died of laughing. Sir John Lambert, one of the most amiable and moral men in the world, said so mildly, "A very large family indeed, Mr. Woodville," that it set Stirling and me off again, and the old patriarch joined in the laugh, with, "Ah, the seed of Abraham would people the earth indeed, if every one of his descendants could show my family."

After a week of great amusement we sailed from Havana. The harbour and entrance are perfectly beautiful: the works most formidable, but the Spaniards would not let us inside. Sailing into the harbour is like entering a large gateway; the sails are almost within reach of the Moro rock, and there is a swell setting into the harbour, which gives the ship a motion, as if every wave would dash her on the Moro.

In the Gulf of Florida we encountered a most terrific gale, wind and current at variance, and oh, such a sea! We lay to for forty-eight hours; we could not cook, and the main deck was flooded. Sir John and I never got out of our cots: he perfectly good-humoured on all occasions, and always convincing himself, and endeavouring to convince us that the gale was abating. The third morning Stirling came to my cot. "Come, turn out; you will see how I manage my craft. I am going to make sail, and our lubberly cut may set us on our beam-ends or sink us altogether." A delightful prospect, indeed. He was and is a noble seaman, all animation and he was so clear and decided in his orders!

Sail was made amid waves mountains high, and the Brazen, as impudent a craft as ever spurned the mighty billows, so beautifully was she managed and steered, rode over or evaded seas apparently over-whelming; and Stirling, in the pride of his sailor's heart, says, "There, now, what would you give to be a sailor?" It really was a sight worth looking at—a little bit of human construction stemming and resisting the power of the mighty deep.

As we neared the mouth of the British Channel, we had, of course, the usual thick weather, when a strange sail was reported. It was now blowing a fresh breeze; in a few minutes we spoke her, but did not make her haul her main-topsail, being a bit of a merchantman. Stirling hailed as we shot past. "Where are you from?"

"Portsmouth."

"Any news?"

"No, none."

The ship was almost out of sight, when we heard, "Ho! Bonaparter's back again on the throne of France."

Such a hurrah as I set up, tossing my hat over my head! "I will be a Lieutenant-Colonel yet before the year's out!"

Sir John Lambert said, "Really, Smith, you are so vivacious! How is it possible? It cannot be." He had such faith in the arrangements of our government, he wouldn't believe it.

I said, "Depend upon it, it's truth; a beast like that skipper never could have invented it, when he did not even regard it as news: 'No, no news; only Bonaparte's back again on the throne of France.' Depend on it, it's true."

"No, Smith, no." Stirling believed it, and oh, how he carried on!

We were soon at Spithead, when all the men-of-war, the bustle, the general appearance, told us, before we could either see telegraphic communication or speak any one, where "Bonaparter" was.

We anchored about three o'clock, went on shore immediately, and shortly after were at dinner in the George. Old West had brought from the Havannah two pups of little white curly dogs, a dog and bitch, which he said were "a present for missus." They are very much esteemed in England, these Havana lapdogs; not much in my way.

The charm of novelty which I experienced on my former visit to England after seven years absence, was much worn off; and I thought of nothing but home. Sir John and I started for London in a chaise at night, and got only as far as Guildford. I soon found our rate of progression would not do, and I asked his leave to set off home. At that time he was not aware of all my tale. I never saw his affectionate heart angry before; he positively scolded me, and said, "I will report our arrival; write to me, that I may know your address, for I shall most probably very soon want you again." My wife and Sir John were afterwards the greatest friends.

So Mr. West and I got a chaise, and off we started, and got to London on a Sunday, the most melancholy place on that day on earth. I drove to my old lodgings, where I had last parted from my wife. They could assure me she was well, as she had very lately ordered a new riding-habit. So I ordered a post-chaise and ran from Panton Square to Weeks' in the Haymarket, and bought a superb dressing-case and a heavy gold chain; I had brought a lot of Spanish books from the Havannah. So on this occasion I did not return to my home naked and penniless, as from Coruña.

I got to Waltham Cross about twelve o'clock. I soon found a pair of horses was far too slow for my galloping ideas; so I got four, and we galloped along then as fast as I could wish. I rattled away to the Falcon Inn in my native place, Whittlesea; for I dare not drive to my father's house. I sent quietly for him, and he was with me in a moment. The people were in church as I drove past. My wife was there, so as yet she was safe from any sudden alarm. She and my sisters took a walk after church, when servants were sent in every direction in search of them, with orders quietly to say that my father wanted my sisters.

A fool of a fellow being the first to find them, and delighted with his prowess, ran up, shouting, "Come home directly; a gentleman has come in a chaise-and-four" who, he did not know. My poor wife, as he named no one, immediately believed someone had arrived to say I was killed, and down she fell senseless. My sisters soon restored her, and they ran home, to their delight, into my arms. My wife and I were never again separated[16], though many an eventful scene was in store and at hand for us.

We were now all happiness. During my few months' absence nothing had occurred to damp their contentment; so we all blessed God Almighty that I had again been protected in such awful situations both by land and sea, while so many families had to grieve for the loss of their dearest relatives. Pug and Tiny recognized me. I heard from Sir John Lambert that he was to be employed with the army assembling at Brussels under the Duke, that I had better be prepared to join him at a few hours' notice, that my position near him would require horses. I knew that "Major of Brigade" was the berth intended for me.

My wife was to accompany me again to the war, but nothing affected us when united; the word "separation" away, all was smooth. All was now excitement, joy, hope and animation,

16. They were separated for a great part of a year during the Kafir War, 1835. Perhaps he is thinking especially of separation by sea.

and preparation of riding-habits, tents, canteens, etc., my sisters thinking of all sorts of things for my wife's comfort, which we could as well have carried as our parish church.

My youngest brother but one, Charles was to go with me as a Volunteer[17], and his departure added to the excitement. I never was more happy in all my life; not a thought of the future (though God knows we had enough before us), for my wife was going and all the agony of parting was spared.

I immediately set to work to buy a real good stud. Two horses I bought at Newmarket, and two in my native place; and as Tiny the faithful was voted too old, as was the mare I had with me in Spain and Washington, I bought for my wife, from a brother, a mare of great celebrity, bred by my father, a perfect horse for a lady who was an equestrian artist.

In a few days I had a kind letter from Sir John Lambert, saying I was appointed his Major of Brigade; and as he was to proceed to Ghent in Flanders, recommending me, being in Cambridgeshire, to proceed *via* Harwich for Ostend, as I must find my own passage unless I went on a transport. West was therefore despatched with my four horses *via* Newmarket for Harwich, and I intended so to start as to be there the day my horses would arrive.

---

17 "During the Peninsular War, and how long before I know not, it was very occasionally permitted to young men who had difficulty in getting a commission, with the consent of the commanding officer, to join some regiment on service before the enemy. In action the Volunteer acted as a private soldier, carrying his musket and wearing his cross-belts like any other man. After a campaign or two, or after having distinguished himself at the storming of some town or fortress, he would probably obtain a commission. He messed with the officers of the company to which he was attached. His dress was the same as that of an officer, except that, instead of wings or epaulettes, he wore shoulder-straps of silver or gold, to confine the cross-belts."—W. Leeke, Lord Seaton's *Regiment at Waterloo* (1866), vol. 1.

Smith, Harry-*Bugler and Officer of the Rifles* (with William Green)

Smith, Harry (with William Surtees)-*The 95th (Rifles) in America*-The experiences of two soldiers during the War of 1812

Surtees, William-*Surtees of the 95th (Rifles)*-A soldier of the 95th (Rifles) in the Peninsular Campaign of the Napoleonic Wars

Surtees, William (with Harry Smith)-*The 95th (Rifles) in America*-The experiences of two soldiers during the War of 1812

Titles about the regiments of the 'Light Division'-43rd & 52nd Foot published by Leonaur

Colborne, John-*Colborne: A Singular Talent for War*-The Napoleonic War career of one of Wellington's most highly valued officers in Egypt, Holland, Italy, The Peninsula and Waterloo (52nd)

Cooke, John.H.-*With the Light Division*-The Experiences of an officer of the 43rd Light Infantry in the Peninsula and South of France during the Napoleonic Wars

Cooke, John.H.-*The Light Infantry Officer*-The Further Adventures of an officer of the 'Light Bobs' (America-War of 1812 -New Orleans)

Dobbs, John-*Gentlemen in Red* (with Robert Knowles)-Recollections of an old 52nd man

Garrety, Thomas-*Soldiering with the 'Division'*, The military experiences of an infantryman of the 43rd regiment during the Napoleonic Wars

Title about the 60th published by Leonaur

Rigeaud, Gibbes-*Swift and Bold*-The 60th Rifles during the Peninsular War

Waterloo-containing the experiences of officers of the 95th and 52nd regiments

Siborne, H.T.-*The Waterloo Letters*-Accounts of the battle by British Officers for its foremost historian

The Rifles Post Waterloo

Cope, William–*The History of the Rifle Brigade Volume 2 1816-1876*
During the Kaffir Wars, The Crimean War,
The Indian Mutiny, The Fenian Uprising and
The Ashanti War

The Leonaur Editors

LEONAUR

ALSO FROM LEONAUR

AVAILABLE IN SOFTCOVER OR HARDCOVER WITH DUST JACKET

A HISTORY OF THE FRENCH & INDIAN WAR *by Arthur G. Bradley*—The Seven Years War as it was fought in the New World has always fascinated students of military history—here is the story of that confrontation.

WASHINGTON'S EARLY CAMPAIGNS *by James Hadden*—The French Post Expedition, Great Meadows and Braddock's Defeat—including Braddock's Orderly Books.

BOUQUET & THE OHIO INDIAN WAR *by Cyrus Cort & William Smith*—Two Accounts of the Campaigns of 1763-1764: Bouquet's Campaigns by Cyrus Cort & The History of Bouquet's Expeditions by William Smith.

NARRATIVES OF THE FRENCH & INDIAN WAR: 2 *by David Holden, Samuel Jenks, Lemuel Lyon, Mary Cochrane Rogers & Henry T. Blake*—Contains The Diary of Sergeant David Holden, Captain Samuel Jenks' Journal, The Journal of Lemuel Lyon, Journal of a French Officer at the Siege of Quebec, A Battle Fought on Snowshoes & The Battle of Lake George.

NARRATIVES OF THE FRENCH & INDIAN WAR *by Brown, Eastburn, Hawks & Putnam*—Ranger Brown's Narrative, The Adventures of Robert Eastburn, The Journal of Rufus Putnam—Provincial Infantry & Orderly Book and Journal of Major John Hawks on the Ticonderoga-Crown Point Campaign.

THE 7TH (QUEEN'S OWN) HUSSARS: Volume 1—1688-1792 *by C. R. B. Barrett*—As Dragoons During the Flanders Campaign, War of the Austrian Succession and the Seven Years War.

INDIA'S FREE LANCES *by H. G. Keene*—European Mercenary Commanders in Hindustan 1770-1820.

THE BENGAL EUROPEAN REGIMENT *by P. R. Innes*—An Elite Regiment of the Honourable East India Company 1756-1858.

MUSKET & TOMAHAWK *by Francis Parkman*—A Military History of the French & Indian War, 1753-1760.

THE BLACK WATCH AT TICONDEROGA *by Frederick B. Richards*—Campaigns in the French & Indian War.

QUEEN'S RANGERS *by Frederick B. Richards*—John Simcoe and his Rangers During the Revolutionary War for America.

LEONAUR

ALSO FROM LEONAUR
AVAILABLE IN SOFTCOVER OR HARDCOVER WITH DUST JACKET

AFGHANISTAN: THE BELEAGUERED BRIGADE *by G. R. Gleig*—An Account of Sale's Brigade During the First Afghan War.

IN THE RANKS OF THE C. I. V *by Erskine Childers*—With the City Imperial Volunteer Battery (Honourable Artillery Company) in the Second Boer War.

THE BENGAL NATIVE ARMY *by F. G. Cardew*—An Invaluable Reference Resource.

THE 7TH (QUEEN'S OWN) HUSSARS: Volume 4—1688-1914 *by C. R. B. Barrett*—Uniforms, Equipment, Weapons, Traditions, the Services of Notable Officers and Men & the Appendices to All Volumes—Volume 4: 1688-1914.

THE SWORD OF THE CROWN *by Eric W. Sheppard*—A History of the British Army to 1914.

THE 7TH (QUEEN'S OWN) HUSSARS: Volume 3—1818-1914 *by C. R. B. Barrett*—On Campaign During the Canadian Rebellion, the Indian Mutiny, the Sudan, Matabeleland, Mashonaland and the Boer War Volume 3: 1818-1914.

THE KHARTOUM CAMPAIGN *by Bennet Burleigh*—A Special Correspondent's View of the Reconquest of the Sudan by British and Egyptian Forces under Kitchener—1898.

EL PUCHERO *by Richard McSherry*—The Letters of a Surgeon of Volunteers During Scott's Campaign of the American-Mexican War 1847-1848.

RIFLEMAN SAHIB *by E. Maude*—The Recollections of an Officer of the Bombay Rifles During the Southern Mahratta Campaign, Second Sikh War, Persian Campaign and Indian Mutiny.

THE KING'S HUSSAR *by Edwin Mole*—The Recollections of a 14th (King's) Hussar During the Victorian Era.

JOHN COMPANY'S CAVALRYMAN *by William Johnson*—The Experiences of a British Soldier in the Crimea, the Persian Campaign and the Indian Mutiny.

COLENSO & DURNFORD'S ZULU WAR *by Frances E. Colenso & Edward Durnford*—The first and possibly the most important history of the Zulu War.

U. S. DRAGOON *by Samuel E. Chamberlain*—Experiences in the Mexican War 1846-48 and on the South Western Frontier.

LEONAUR

ALSO FROM LEONAUR
AVAILABLE IN SOFTCOVER OR HARDCOVER WITH DUST JACKET

AT THEM WITH THE BAYONET *by Donald F. Featherstone*—The first Anglo-Sikh War 1845-1846.

STEPHEN CRANE'S BATTLES *by Stephen Crane*—Nine Decisive Battles Recounted by the Author of 'The Red Badge of Courage'.

THE GURKHA WAR *by H. T. Prinsep*—The Anglo-Nepalese Conflict in North East India 1814-1816.

FIRE & BLOOD *by G. R. Gleig*—The burning of Washington & the battle of New Orleans, 1814, through the eyes of a young British soldier.

SOUND ADVANCE! *by Joseph Anderson*—Experiences of an officer of HM 50th regiment in Australia, Burma & the Gwalior war.

THE CAMPAIGN OF THE INDUS *by Thomas Holdsworth*—Experiences of a British Officer of the 2nd (Queen's Royal) Regiment in the Campaign to Place Shah Shuja on the Throne of Afghanistan 1838 - 1840.

WITH THE MADRAS EUROPEAN REGIMENT IN BURMA *by John Butler*—The Experiences of an Officer of the Honourable East India Company's Army During the First Anglo-Burmese War 1824 - 1826.

IN ZULULAND WITH THE BRITISH ARMY *by Charles L. Norris-Newman*—The Anglo-Zulu war of 1879 through the first-hand experiences of a special correspondent.

BESIEGED IN LUCKNOW *by Martin Richard Gubbins*—The first Anglo-Sikh War 1845-1846.

A TIGER ON HORSEBACK *by L. March Phillips*—The Experiences of a Trooper & Officer of Rimington's Guides - The Tigers - during the Anglo-Boer war 1899 - 1902.

SEPOYS, SIEGE & STORM *by Charles John Griffiths*—The Experiences of a young officer of H.M.'s 61st Regiment at Ferozepore, Delhi ridge and at the fall of Delhi during the Indian mutiny 1857.

CAMPAIGNING IN ZULULAND *by W. E. Montague*—Experiences on campaign during the Zulu war of 1879 with the 94th Regiment.

THE STORY OF THE GUIDES *by G.J. Younghusband*—The Exploits of the Soldiers of the famous Indian Army Regiment from the northwest frontier 1847 - 1900.

LEONAUR

ALSO FROM LEONAUR
AVAILABLE IN SOFTCOVER OR HARDCOVER WITH DUST JACKET

ZULU:1879 *by D.C.F. Moodie & the Leonaur Editors*—The Anglo-Zulu War of 1879 from contemporary sources: First Hand Accounts, Interviews, Dispatches, Official Documents & Newspaper Reports.

THE RED DRAGOON *by W.J. Adams*—With the 7th Dragoon Guards in the Cape of Good Hope against the Boers & the Kaffir tribes during the 'war of the axe' 1843-48'.

THE RECOLLECTIONS OF SKINNER OF SKINNER'S HORSE *by James Skinner*—James Skinner and his 'Yellow Boys' Irregular cavalry in the wars of India between the British, Mahratta, Rajput, Mogul, Sikh & Pindarree Forces.

A CAVALRY OFFICER DURING THE SEPOY REVOLT *by A. R. D. Mackenzie*—Experiences with the 3rd Bengal Light Cavalry, the Guides and Sikh Irregular Cavalry from the outbreak to Delhi and Lucknow.

A NORFOLK SOLDIER IN THE FIRST SIKH WAR *by J W Baldwin*—Experiences of a private of H.M. 9th Regiment of Foot in the battles for the Punjab, India 1845-6.

TOMMY ATKINS' WAR STORIES: 14 FIRST HAND ACCOUNTS—Fourteen first hand accounts from the ranks of the British Army during Queen Victoria's Empire.

THE WATERLOO LETTERS *by H. T. Siborne*—Accounts of the Battle by British Officers for its Foremost Historian.

NEY: GENERAL OF CAVALRY VOLUME 1—1769-1799 *by Antoine Bulos*—The Early Career of a Marshal of the First Empire.

NEY: MARSHAL OF FRANCE VOLUME 2—1799-1805 *by Antoine Bulos*—The Early Career of a Marshal of the First Empire.

AIDE-DE-CAMP TO NAPOLEON *by Philippe-Paul de Ségur*—For anyone interested in the Napoleonic Wars this book, written by one who was intimate with the strategies and machinations of the Emperor, will be essential reading.

TWILIGHT OF EMPIRE *by Sir Thomas Ussher & Sir George Cockburn*—Two accounts of Napoleon's Journeys in Exile to Elba and St. Helena: Narrative of Events by Sir Thomas Ussher & Napoleon's Last Voyage: Extract of a diary by Sir George Cockburn.

PRIVATE WHEELER *by William Wheeler*—The letters of a soldier of the 51st Light Infantry during the Peninsular War & at Waterloo.

LEONAUR

ALSO FROM LEONAUR
AVAILABLE IN SOFTCOVER OR HARDCOVER WITH DUST JACKET

COLBORNE: A SINGULAR TALENT FOR WAR *by John Colborne*—The Napoleonic Wars Career of One of Wellington's Most Highly Valued Officers in Egypt, Holland, Italy, the Peninsula and at Waterloo.

NAPOLEON'S RUSSIAN CAMPAIGN *by Philippe Henri de Segur*—The Invasion, Battles and Retreat by an Aide-de-Camp on the Emperor's Staff.

WITH THE LIGHT DIVISION *by John H. Cooke*—The Experiences of an Officer of the 43rd Light Infantry in the Peninsula and South of France During the Napoleonic Wars.

WELLINGTON AND THE PYRENEES CAMPAIGN VOLUME I: FROM VITORIA TO THE BIDASSOA *by F. C. Beatson*—The final phase of the campaign in the Iberian Peninsula.

WELLINGTON AND THE INVASION OF FRANCE VOLUME II: THE BIDASSOA TO THE BATTLE OF THE NIVELLE *by F. C. Beatson*—The final phase of the campaign in the Iberian Peninsula.

WELLINGTON AND THE FALL OF FRANCE VOLUME III: THE GAVES AND THE BATTLE OF ORTHEZ *by F. C. Beatson*—The final phase of the campaign in the Iberian Peninsula.

NAPOLEON'S IMPERIAL GUARD: FROM MARENGO TO WATERLOO *by J. T. Headley*—The story of Napoleon's Imperial Guard and the men who commanded them.

BATTLES & SIEGES OF THE PENINSULAR WAR *by W. H. Fitchett*—Corunna, Busaco, Albuera, Ciudad Rodrigo, Badajos, Salamanca, San Sebastian & Others.

SERGEANT GUILLEMARD: THE MAN WHO SHOT NELSON? *by Robert Guillemard*—A Soldier of the Infantry of the French Army of Napoleon on Campaign Throughout Europe.

WITH THE GUARDS ACROSS THE PYRENEES *by Robert Batty*—The Experiences of a British Officer of Wellington's Army During the Battles for the Fall of Napoleonic France, 1813 .

A STAFF OFFICER IN THE PENINSULA *by E. W. Buckham*—An Officer of the British Staff Corps Cavalry During the Peninsula Campaign of the Napoleonic Wars.

THE LEIPZIG CAMPAIGN: 1813—NAPOLEON AND THE "BATTLE OF THE NATIONS" *by F. N. Maude*—Colonel Maude's analysis of Napoleon's campaign of 1813 around Leipzig.

LEONAUR
ALSO FROM LEONAUR
AVAILABLE IN SOFTCOVER OR HARDCOVER WITH DUST JACKET

CAPTAIN COIGNET *by Jean-Roch Coignet*—A Soldier of Napoleon's Imperial Guard from the Italian Campaign to Russia and Waterloo.

HUSSAR ROCCA *by Albert Jean Michel de Rocca*—A French cavalry officer's experiences of the Napoleonic Wars and his views on the Peninsular Campaigns against the Spanish, British And Guerilla Armies.

MARINES TO 95TH (RIFLES) *by Thomas Fernyhough*—The military experiences of Robert Fernyhough during the Napoleonic Wars.

LIGHT BOB *by Robert Blakeney*—The experiences of a young officer in H.M 28th & 36th regiments of the British Infantry during the Peninsular Campaign of the Napoleonic Wars 1804 - 1814.

WITH WELLINGTON'S LIGHT CAVALRY *by William Tomkinson*—The Experiences of an officer of the 16th Light Dragoons in the Peninsular and Waterloo campaigns of the Napoleonic Wars.

SERGEANT BOURGOGNE *by Adrien Bourgogne*—With Napoleon's Imperial Guard in the Russian Campaign and on the Retreat from Moscow 1812 - 13.

SURTEES OF THE 95TH (RIFLES) *by William Surtees*—A Soldier of the 95th (Rifles) in the Peninsular campaign of the Napoleonic Wars.

SWORDS OF HONOUR *by Henry Newbolt & Stanley L. Wood*—The Careers of Six Outstanding Officers from the Napoleonic Wars, the Wars for India and the American Civil War.

ENSIGN BELL IN THE PENINSULAR WAR *by George Bell*—The Experiences of a young British Soldier of the 34th Regiment 'The Cumberland Gentlemen' in the Napoleonic wars.

HUSSAR IN WINTER *by Alexander Gordon*—A British Cavalry Officer during the retreat to Corunna in the Peninsular campaign of the Napoleonic Wars.

THE COMPLEAT RIFLEMAN HARRIS *by Benjamin Harris as told to and transcribed by Captain Henry Curling, 52nd Regt. of Foot*—The adventures of a soldier of the 95th (Rifles) during the Peninsular Campaign of the Napoleonic Wars.

THE ADVENTURES OF A LIGHT DRAGOON *by George Farmer & G.R. Gleig*—A cavalryman during the Peninsular & Waterloo Campaigns, in captivity & at the siege of Bhurtpore, India.

LEONAUR

ALSO FROM LEONAUR
AVAILABLE IN SOFTCOVER OR HARDCOVER WITH DUST JACKET

THE LIFE OF THE REAL BRIGADIER GERARD VOLUME 1—THE YOUNG HUSSAR 1782-1807 *by Jean-Baptiste De Marbot*—A French Cavalryman Of the Napoleonic Wars at Marengo, Austerlitz, Jena, Eylau & Friedland.

THE LIFE OF THE REAL BRIGADIER GERARD VOLUME 2—IMPERIAL AIDE-DE-CAMP 1807-1811 *by Jean-Baptiste De Marbot*—A French Cavalryman of the Napoleonic Wars at Saragossa, Landshut, Eckmuhl, Ratisbon, Aspern-Essling, Wagram, Busaco & Torres Vedras.

THE LIFE OF THE REAL BRIGADIER GERARD VOLUME 3—COLONEL OF CHASSEURS 1811-1815 *by Jean-Baptiste De Marbot*—A French Cavalryman in the retreat from Moscow, Lutzen, Bautzen, Katzbach, Leipzig, Hanau & Waterloo.

THE INDIAN WAR OF 1864 *by Eugene Ware*—The Experiences of a Young Officer of the 7th Iowa Cavalry on the Western Frontier During the Civil War.

THE MARCH OF DESTINY *by Charles E. Young & V. Devinny*—Dangers of the Trail in 1865 by Charles E. Young & The Story of a Pioneer by V. Devinny, two Accounts of Early Emigrants to Colorado.

CROSSING THE PLAINS *by William Audley Maxwell*—A First Hand Narrative of the Early Pioneer Trail to California in 1857.

CHIEF OF SCOUTS *by William F. Drannan*—A Pilot to Emigrant and Government Trains, Across the Plains of the Western Frontier.

THIRTY-ONE YEARS ON THE PLAINS AND IN THE MOUNTAINS *by William F. Drannan*—William Drannan was born to be a pioneer, hunter, trapper and wagon train guide during the momentous days of the Great American West.

THE INDIAN WARS VOLUNTEER *by William Thompson*—Recollections of the Conflict Against the Snakes, Shoshone, Bannocks, Modocs and Other Native Tribes of the American North West.

THE 4TH TENNESSEE CAVALRY *by George B. Guild*—The Services of Smith's Regiment of Confederate Cavalry by One of its Officers.

COLONEL WORTHINGTON'S SHILOH *by T. Worthington*—The Tennessee Campaign, 1862, by an Officer of the Ohio Volunteers.

FOUR YEARS IN THE SADDLE *by W. L. Curry*—The History of the First Regiment Ohio Volunteer Cavalry in the American Civil War.

LEONAUR

ALSO FROM LEONAUR

AVAILABLE IN SOFTCOVER OR HARDCOVER WITH DUST JACKET

ESCAPE FROM THE FRENCH *by Edward Boys*—A Young Royal Navy Midshipman's Adventures During the Napoleonic War.

THE VOYAGE OF H.M.S. PANDORA *by Edward Edwards R. N. & George Hamilton, edited by Basil Thomson*—In Pursuit of the Mutineers of the Bounty in the South Seas—1790-1791.

MEDUSA *by J. B. Henry Savigny and Alexander Correard and Charlotte-Adélaïde Dard* —Narrative of a Voyage to Senegal in 1816 & The Sufferings of the Picard Family After the Shipwreck of the Medusa.

THE SEA WAR OF 1812 VOLUME 1 *by A. T. Mahan*—A History of the Maritime Conflict.

THE SEA WAR OF 1812 VOLUME 2 *by A. T. Mahan*—A History of the Maritime Conflict.

WETHERELL OF H. M. S. HUSSAR *by John Wetherell*—The Recollections of an Ordinary Seaman of the Royal Navy During the Napoleonic Wars.

THE NAVAL BRIGADE IN NATAL *by C. R. N. Burne*—With the Guns of H. M. S. Terrible & H. M. S. Tartar during the Boer War 1899-1900.

THE VOYAGE OF H. M. S. BOUNTY *by William Bligh*—The True Story of an 18th Century Voyage of Exploration and Mutiny.

SHIPWRECK! *by William Gilly*—The Royal Navy's Disasters at Sea 1793-1849.

KING'S CUTTERS AND SMUGGLERS: 1700-1855 *by E. Keble Chatterton*—A unique period of maritime history-from the beginning of the eighteenth to the middle of the nineteenth century when British seamen risked all to smuggle valuable goods from wool to tea and spirits from and to the Continent.

CONFEDERATE BLOCKADE RUNNER *by John Wilkinson*—The Personal Recollections of an Officer of the Confederate Navy.

NAVAL BATTLES OF THE NAPOLEONIC WARS *by W. H. Fitchett*—Cape St. Vincent, the Nile, Cadiz, Copenhagen, Trafalgar & Others.

PRISONERS OF THE RED DESERT *by R. S. Gwatkin-Williams*—The Adventures of the Crew of the Tara During the First World War.

U-BOAT WAR 1914-1918 *by James B. Connolly/Karl von Schenk*—Two Contrasting Accounts from Both Sides of the Conflict at Sea During the Great War.

LEONAUR

ALSO FROM LEONAUR

AVAILABLE IN SOFTCOVER OR HARDCOVER WITH DUST JACKET

IRON TIMES WITH THE GUARDS *by An O. E. (G. P. A. Fildes)*—The Experiences of an Officer of the Coldstream Guards on the Western Front During the First World War.

THE GREAT WAR IN THE MIDDLE EAST: 1 *by W. T. Massey*—The Desert Campaigns & How Jerusalem Was Won---two classic accounts in one volume.

THE GREAT WAR IN THE MIDDLE EAST: 2 *by W. T. Massey*—Allenby's Final Triumph.

SMITH-DORRIEN *by Horace Smith-Dorrien*—Isandlwhana to the Great War.

1914 *by Sir John French*—The Early Campaigns of the Great War by the British Commander.

GRENADIER *by E. R. M. Fryer*—The Recollections of an Officer of the Grenadier Guards throughout the Great War on the Western Front.

BATTLE, CAPTURE & ESCAPE *by George Pearson*—The Experiences of a Canadian Light Infantryman During the Great War.

DIGGERS AT WAR *by R. Hugh Knyvett & G. P. Cuttriss*—"Over There" With the Australians by R. Hugh Knyvett and Over the Top With the Third Australian Division by G. P. Cuttriss. Accounts of Australians During the Great War in the Middle East, at Gallipoli and on the Western Front.

HEAVY FIGHTING BEFORE US *by George Brenton Laurie*—The Letters of an Officer of the Royal Irish Rifles on the Western Front During the Great War.

THE CAMELIERS *by Oliver Hogue*—A Classic Account of the Australians of the Imperial Camel Corps During the First World War in the Middle East.

RED DUST *by Donald Black*—A Classic Account of Australian Light Horsemen in Palestine During the First World War.

THE LEAN, BROWN MEN *by Angus Buchanan*—Experiences in East Africa During the Great War with the 25th Royal Fusiliers—the Legion of Frontiersmen.

THE NIGERIAN REGIMENT IN EAST AFRICA *by W. D. Downes*—On Campaign During the Great War 1916-1918.

THE 'DIE-HARDS' IN SIBERIA *by John Ward*—With the Middlesex Regiment Against the Bolsheviks 1918-19.

LEONAUR

ALSO FROM LEONAUR
AVAILABLE IN SOFTCOVER OR HARDCOVER WITH DUST JACKET

FARAWAY CAMPAIGN *by F. James*—Experiences of an Indian Army Cavalry Officer in Persia & Russia During the Great War.

REVOLT IN THE DESERT *by T. E. Lawrence*—An account of the experiences of one remarkable British officer's war from his own perspective.

MACHINE-GUN SQUADRON *by A. M. G.*—The 20th Machine Gunners from British Yeomanry Regiments in the Middle East Campaign of the First World War.

A GUNNER'S CRUSADE *by Antony Bluett*—The Campaign in the Desert, Palestine & Syria as Experienced by the Honourable Artillery Company During the Great War .

DESPATCH RIDER *by W. H. L. Watson*—The Experiences of a British Army Motorcycle Despatch Rider During the Opening Battles of the Great War in Europe.

TIGERS ALONG THE TIGRIS *by E. J. Thompson*—The Leicestershire Regiment in Mesopotamia During the First World War.

HEARTS & DRAGONS *by Charles R. M. F. Crutwell*—The 4th Royal Berkshire Regiment in France and Italy During the Great War, 1914-1918.

INFANTRY BRIGADE: 1914 *by John Ward*—The Diary of a Commander of the 15th Infantry Brigade, 5th Division, British Army, During the Retreat from Mons.

DOING OUR 'BIT' *by Ian Hay*—Two Classic Accounts of the Men of Kitchener's 'New Army' During the Great War including *The First 100,000* & *All In It*.

AN EYE IN THE STORM *by Arthur Ruhl*—An American War Correspondent's Experiences of the First World War from the Western Front to Gallipoli-and Beyond.

STAND & FALL *by Joe Cassells*—With the Middlesex Regiment Against the Bolsheviks 1918-19.

RIFLEMAN MACGILL'S WAR *by Patrick MacGill*—A Soldier of the London Irish During the Great War in Europe including *The Amateur Army*, *The Red Horizon* & *The Great Push*.

WITH THE GUNS *by C. A. Rose & Hugh Dalton*—Two First Hand Accounts of British Gunners at War in Europe During World War 1- Three Years in France with the Guns and With the British Guns in Italy.

THE BUSH WAR DOCTOR *by Robert V. Dolbey*—The Experiences of a British Army Doctor During the East African Campaign of the First World War.